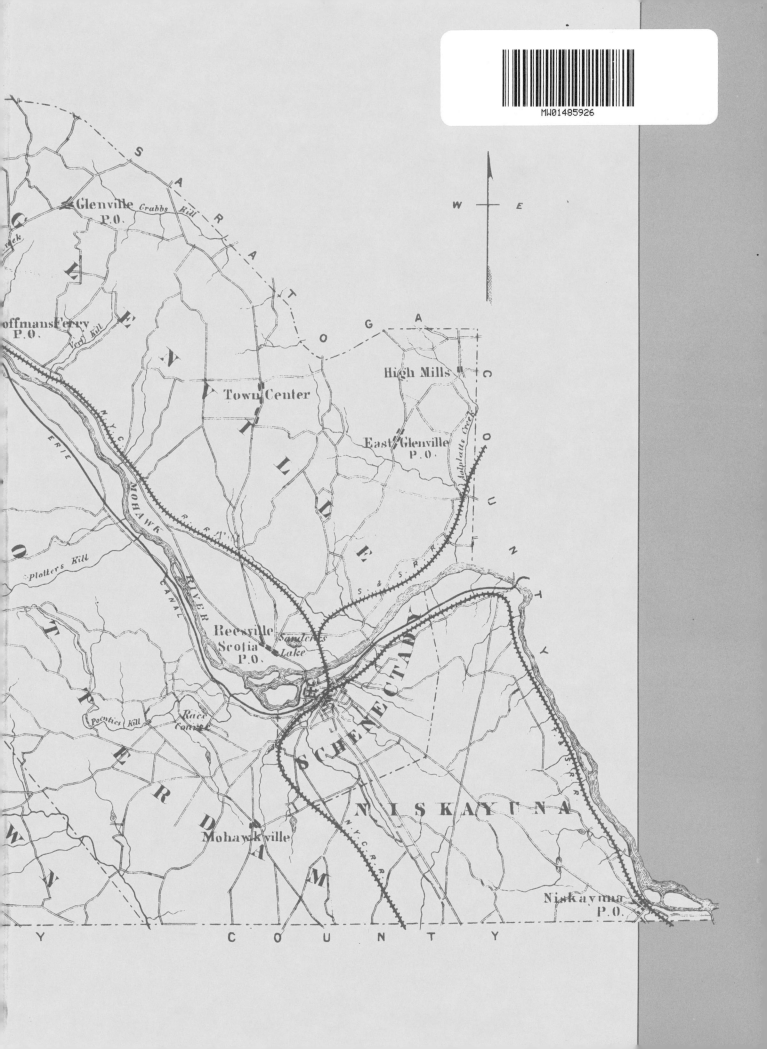

Glenville
P.O.
Crabbs Kill

S A R A T O G A     C O U N T Y

offmans Ferry
P.O.

High Mills

Town Center

East Glenville
P.O.

ERIE

N.Y.C.R.R.

Mohawk

CANAL

Plotters Kill

S & S R R

RIVER

Reesville
Scotia
P.O.
Sanders
Lake

SCHENECTADY

Poenties Kill

Race
Course

N I S K A Y U N A

Mohawkville

N.Y.C.R.R.

Niskayuna
P.O.

C O U N T Y

W — E

*This photo from 1926 shows the original bank building. The structure still serves as the main office, with many additions having been made to it over the years, of course.* (Photo by White Studio, Schenectady)

We at 1st National Bank of Scotia are most pleased and honored to make available this reprinted edition of Larry Hart's 1987 book *Schenectady: Changing with the Times* for readers in 2005. As one of the few remaining independent banks in the Schenectady area, it is the bank's wish to be sure that this type of local history is preserved and passed on to the next generation.

Our respect for Larry Hart's work runs deep. He's done so much to further everyone's knowledge of the history of Glenville, it is right to make sure that this book is available again. Also, we strongly believe in the Schenectady County Historical Society and its efforts to protect the history of Schenectady County.

Established in 1923, we were the first bank in Schenectady County to be located outside the city of Schenectady. Schenectady County is important to this bank and we have a commitment to it, so we feel it's our responsibility to further the knowledge of local history so that it is never forgotten. We are pleased to be the sponsor of the reprint of this volume by Larry Hart.

*Kenneth E. Buhrmaster,*
*Chairman of 1st National Bank of Scotia since 1952*

1ST
NATIONAL
BANK OF
SCOTIA MEMBER FDIC
*The Family Bank*

HARGREAVES & CO.
201 TAILORS 201

PEOPLE'S

207

MILLINERY NEW YORK BAZAAR FURS

203 CLOAKS NEW YORK BAZAAR SUITS ETC.

NEW YORK BAZAAR STORES

H. S. BARNEY CO.

THE H. S. BARNEY COMPANY

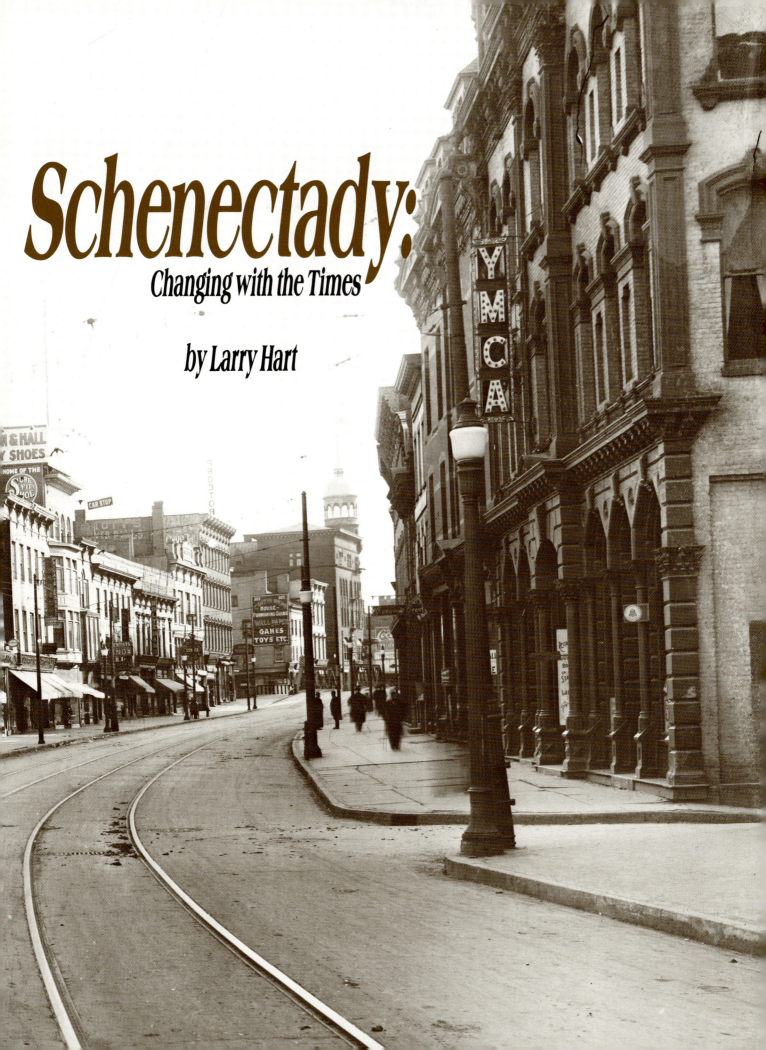

# Schenectady:
## Changing with the Times

*by Larry Hart*

**LARRY HART BOOK LIST**

| | |
|---|---|
| The Sacandaga Story | $6.50 |
| Schenectady's Golden Era | $19.95 |
| Did I Wake You Up? | $8.00 |
| Tales of Old Schenectady, Vol. 1 | $15.00 |
| Tales of Old Schenectady, Vol. 2 | $15.00 |
| Schenectady: A Pictorial History | $16.95 |
| Best of Old Dorp, Book One | $16.95 |
| Through the Darkest Hour | $10.00 |
| Schenectady: Facts & Stuff (Booklet) | $1.75 |
| Pictures From the Past | $15.00 |
| This I Remember…Growing Up In Schenectady | $15.00 |
| ALCO Booklet | $3.00 |

**RUTH HART BOOK LIST**

| | |
|---|---|
| Blabbermouth | $10.00 |

**ALAN HART BOOK LIST**

| | |
|---|---|
| Larry Hart, My Dad | $14.00 |
| Dear Old Scotia | $18.00 |

To order any of the aforementioned books, please include $3 per book for handling.

Mail to:
**Old Dorp Books**
**120 Waters Road**
**Scotia, New York 12302**

Or call:
**(518) 887-5789**

The Donning Company Publishers
184 Business Park Drive, Suite 206
Virginia Beach, VA 23462

Steve Mull, General Manager
Barbara Buchanan, Office Manager
Sharon Varner Moyer, Graphic Designer
Amy E. M. Kouba, Editor
Richard A. Horwege, Senior Editor
Pamela Koch, Reprint Editor
Lynn Parrott, Reprint Graphic Designer
Stephanie Bass, Imaging Artist
Mary Ellen Wheeler, Proofreader
Susan Adams, Project Research Coordinator
Scott Rule, Director of Marketing
Stephanie Linneman, Marketing Coordinator

**Mary Taylor, Project Director**

**Library of Congress Cataloging-in-Publication Data**
Hart, Larry.
    Schenectady: changing with the times.

    Includes index.
    1. Schenectady (N.Y.)—History—Pictorial works. I. Title.
F129.S5H26     1988     974.7'44     87-38141
ISBN 0-89865-632-X

Printed in the United States of America at Walsworth Publishing Company

*Dust jacket artwork depicts the lower end of State Street in Schenectady in 1832 according to an oil painting by Cornelius Van Patten. Courtesy of Schenectady County Historical Society.*

# Contents

Much about Schenectady County has changed since my late father, Larry Hart, wrote this book, *Schenectady: Changing with the Times*, in 1987.

Yes, eighteen years later in 2005, we find that much of the scenery and many aspects concerning the demographics and sociology of this unique area of upstate New York differ from the circumstances as they were when Dad worked on this fine volume.

For example, any Schenectady resident who picks up this book and begins studying the pages will find fault from time to time. He or she will look at the photograph of the building containing the Key Bank and PriceChopper market on Eastern Avenue on page 79 and say, "Why, this picture is wrong. That's not how the building looks today!" That reader would be correct. That scene, and many others found in the 210 pages which make up this book, has changed since 1987.

When the Donning Company approached my mother (Larry's widow), Ruth Hart, in March of 2005 with the proposal to reprint my father's book, she was most eager to see Dad's book reprinted. It is my mother's wish as well as the entire family's to reprint it just as he wrote it eighteen years ago with this dedication page serving as a disclaimer or reminder to all readers that much about any community in the United States has no doubt changed in just short of the score of years which have passed.

Therefore, it is the Hart family's pleasure to give thousands of new readers a chance to enjoy Larry Hart's *Schenectady: Changing with the Times* just as it was written. Dad no doubt would have duly noted and enjoyed the changes which have occurred in Schenectady County just in this year alone—the improvements up and down State Street to make it more pedestrian-friendly; the enlargement of the stage at great, old Proctor's Theater downtown—just to name two.

Life seldom offers us second chances, so we hope that you will savor this second opportunity to read my father's book on Schenectady County history. We hope you like it, and we have a feeling you will! After all, history never gets old!

Alan Hart (June 2005)

*This view of the MVP building looking east alongside Veterans Park shows how downtown city sidewalks have been widened and beautified to become more pedestrian-friendly.*

# Preface

Having lived in the Schenectady area from the day I was born at 10 Barrett Street in 1920, I am among that rather select group who can say with any authority that most everything in what is affectionately called Old Dorp has changed drastically through the years—ourselves included.

Gone are the old slate sidewalks, fancy wrought-iron fences, the horses and their watering troughs, the neighborhood movie houses, some vacant lots where kids could play scrub baseball, nickel hot dogs and ice cream, steam locomotives and trolley cars, houses with front porches, a busy downtown business district, the peddlers and their wagons, and so on. But I have been on hand to see these changes, not only in the way people live but in the places they live. One can only imagine the shock of former residents who come home after being away many years and feel like strangers in their old home town.

However, let's be realistic. Time does change all things and those who resist change are fighting a losing battle. Yes, we would like to cling forever to that which is familiar, comfortable to our life style, but fate dictates otherwise and we bend with the times. If we stop to think about it, change is not all bad. It's been going on a long time. Back in 1927, when the first "talkie" was produced on screen, I recall our Uncle Jim throwing up his arms in amazement as he blurted, "What'll they think of next?"

In presenting this then-and-now pictorial on the Schenectady area, it is not so much our intention to wax nostalgic as to show the passing scene through existing photographs. Through them we can glimpse the gradual, often imperceptible transpositions in our very own neighborhoods. Those of us who are old enough can remark, just as our forebears did, "How times have changed!" Those who are younger can look at how it was and ponder, "How ever did people cope with those times?"

Larry Hart

1

*This was the lower end of State Street in the 1870s as viewed from Church Street, west toward the river. At the very end is the Freeman House and other buildings that stretched along the river bank. In the foreground is the house of Dr. I. W. Ferris, one of Schenectady's physicians of that period. At left is the beginning of Water Street.*

*The same view as it looks today, with Church Street in the foreground, Water Street in the left background, and the beginning of the Western Gateway Bridge in the far right background where the* *Freeman House once stood. The houses in the triangular plot at left center were pulled down in 1925 and in their place was established Liberty Park.*

# On Lower State Street

Probably nowhere else in the city of Schenectady have there been such drastic physical changes in so many periods of its history—dating back, in fact, from the time of its settlement in 1661—as that portion of State Street from the Mohawk River one block eastward to Church Street.

The north side of State Street once formed the south wall of the original stockade from Washington Avenue up to Ferry Street, but it became an important thoroughfare to complement the fine homes of that historic area after the stockade "fence" was pulled down following the American Revolution. Likewise, the foot of State Street and the south side underwent many changes through the years as will be seen in the following pages.

## Frog Alley

Old-time residents of Schenectady always referred to the area south of lower State Street as "Frog Alley," certainly a term of endearment to those who lived in the area. Probably, from the description given by those who grew up there many years ago, Frog Alley encompassed a triangular section bordered by Washington Avenue, the Erie Canal (now Erie Boulevard) and State Street. This took in a number of side streets, including old Water Street, Railroad Street, Mill Lane, Erie Street, Fuller Street, South Church Street and South Ferry Street.

It was said that the neighborhood got its name from the fact that big bullfrogs were abundant in the marshy area once around Fuller Street and the canal—so profuse that men and boys caught them regularly to sell to the many hotels in the area for "frog's legs" in season.

Originally, Washington Avenue south of State Street was called Rotterdam Street because it led to Rotterdam via the old river road west beside the canal or across Weaver Street to the Broadway hill.

*This was the heart of the Frog Alley section of downtown about 1885, looking down old Rotterdam Street (later to be called Washington Avenue) at the junction of Water Street. Workers are paving the street with cobblestones. Cyrus Scrafford's hotel is just down the street at left center. This is a southerly view, toward the Erie Canal bridge.*

*Spring flooding was common along the river before the building of the Barge Canal and the lock system after 1915, but Frog Alley residents were especially used to it. It was an old saying that "If you're going to live in Frog Alley, you'd better own a rowboat!" The scene below is during the March 1914 flooding as General Electric employees standing near State Street survey a watery Washington Avenue and wonder about getting to work. Water Street, aptly named, crosses in the center background.*

*This photo of June 29, 1926, shows a widened Washington Avenue complete with new street lighting. Houses on the right side were demolished and the west end of Water Street was taken over by the Van Curler Hotel construction. The opening of the rejuvenated Washington Avenue was coordinated with that of Erie Boulevard the previous year.*

*The same view as it looks today.*

Construction of Schenectady's Van Curler
Hotel coincided with that of the first
Western Gateway Bridge, as shown in this
mid-1924 picture. The approach to the
bridge is at right. The hotel opened May 30,
1925, while the bridge traffic began on
December 19 that year.

The hotel closed in February 1968 but
reopened as the Schenectady County
Community College in September 1969.
The bridge entrance, still at right, is to a
new bridge opened in 1973.

In 1936, when this picture was made from the bend in the first Western Gateway Bridge, work was progressing on the new State Armory on Washington Avenue in the right background. The back of the Van Curler Hotel is at left. Fill was being trucked in to grade and enlarge its parking lot. The Binnekill, a tributary of the Mohawk River, is in the foreground.

Now, more than a half century later, the scene has changed greatly. The Binnekill has been filled in to accommodate the growing Schenectady County Community College. The second Western Gateway Bridge at left is partially over land fill on the Schenectady side and ramps have been provided for easy access and egress for college parking.

This aerial view from the foot of State Street, looking northwest toward Scotia, shows the development of the community college campus (center) over what was once the Binnekill. The state armory is at lower right. Courtesy of Schenectady County Community College

The lower end of State Street in
Schenectady looked like this in 1832,
according to an oil painting by Cornelius
Van Patten, who was born in Schenectady
and lived his entire life there. Of his three
known paintings, this was his earliest work.
The small white building to the right was
the law office of John Isaac DeGraff.
Courtesy of Schenectady County Historical
Society

For many years this dignified residence at
13 State Street was the home of James A.
Goodrich, a Schenectady lawyer. It was
demolished after 1923 when Goodrich sold
the property to Schenectady YMCA for its
new headquarters.

*This was the new YMCA building a few months after its dedication in 1928. Actually, it was completed and in use by late 1927.*

*The Schenectady YMCA building is now in its 60th year and remains a popular recreational and physical fitness center for many in the area. Its programs have long since been updated to include family programs for men, women and children on its weekly agenda.*

A number of architectural changes have been made to the two-story brick building at the corner of Church and State streets since it was built in 1762 for Daniel Campbell after plans by Samuel Fuller, a well-known colonial architect. The above view is of the Campbell house in the mid-1800s. To the right, the smaller brick building then housed the Schenectady Bank which was organized in 1832 and became the Schenectady Trust Company in 1902. Campbell came to the colonies from Ireland in 1754, soon settled in Schenectady and became a successful businessman in fur trading.

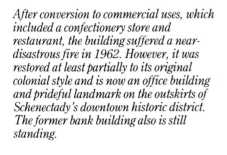

By the 1880s, when this photo was made, the Campbell house had undergone some alterations—including some Victorian embellishments to the exterior. It is shown at left, on the corner of Church Street, looking up State Street into the shopping district.

After conversion to commercial uses, which included a confectionery store and restaurant, the building suffered a near-disastrous fire in 1962. However, it was restored at least partially to its original colonial style and is now an office building and prideful landmark on the outskirts of Schenectady's downtown historic district. The former bank building also is still standing.

*Symbols of the mid-1800s are ever present in this photograph of lower State Street in Schenectady, looking west past Ferry Street at right center. Storefronts all have boardwalk entrances, the sidewalks are paved with brick, the street with cobblestones. Hitching posts are at curbside, a wood cover is over a street cistern at left foreground, an oil street lamp is on the corner across the street, trees line the main street, and the traffic is horse-driven.*

*The same street, the same vantage point, as it looks today, more than a century later.*

Life was slow and leisurely but business was good in downtown Schenectady about 1875 when this picture was made on a wet plate by early photographer Henry Tripp, who once roamed the area in a horse-drawn darkroom. The view is easterly up State Street from the North Ferry Street corner at left. Lewis Behr's tailor and men's clothing shop is at left, while three doors up on the same side is the early department store of Howland S. Barney who started his own business in 1855.

This is the same location in 1915. Now there are trolley tracks over paved macadam and electric street lights instead of gas lamps. Many of the structures built in the early 1800s, still remain, however.

A greater change is evident today, but the bend in the road is unmistakable. There are only a few of the original buildings remaining, including those to the left and several across the street. The former Barney store building recently was converted into a condominium and office complex known as Barney Square.

## A Century of Change

The following pictures, six of them, are a composite example of how one small area was affected by time—from 1875 to today.

It happens to be the northeasterly view of State Street from about the area of the railroad tracks, from the front of the *Schenectady Gazette* building. It shows the metamorphic development of a part of a city's main street, in a way representative of the whole.

Everything was subject to change: the paving, street lighting, transportation, street names, buildings, types of businesses, and most certainly the way in which people dress.

*Schenectady east of the railroad tracks on State Street was principally inns and liveries when this picture was made about 1875. In the center background is the Carley House, formerly the Eagle Hotel. In years to come, it would become the Barhydt House and the Vendome Hotel. The streets had recently been paved with cobblestone up to Lafayette Street. The church steeple in the background, right of center, is that of the First Methodist Church at Lafayette Street, completed in 1874.*

*Downtown Schenectady was a lively place in 1900, as is evident by this photograph at the corner of State Street and Centre Street (now Broadway). The traffic looked to be either by trolley cars or horse and carriage, with a bicycle here and there...and, of course, plenty of pedestrians.*

# Rebuilding Downtown

Downtown Schenectady is like most urban shopping sections of cities across our nation. It has certainly known better days.

Its heyday may have been the period between 1900 and 1930. There was the greatest incidence of new business added to the old established firms, which took up all available space between lower State Street up to the park at Lafayette Street. And most of the merchants on side streets adjoining the main stem enjoyed fringe benefits.

It was not long after the crippling Great Depression and World War II that suburban growth led to suburban malls. By the mid-1950s, its effect was felt up and down the city's shopping core. As downtown business declined so did the appearance of the shops and the general atmosphere of an area that once teemed with people. In the late 1960s and early 1970s, some of the stalwarts of downtown stores closed, most prominent of which were the H. S.

Barney Company, boasting a tenure dating back to 1820, and the Wallace Company, an offshoot of a business that started in 1883.

It was in the mid-1970s that community leaders took definitive action, organizing a group known as FOCUS and engaging famed architect Arthur Cotton Moore to aid in reconstructing downtown buildings and putting them to use. Canal Square was developed in the south 400 block of State Street, part of Jay Street became a pedestrian mall, and several huge empty buildings were converted into apartments and offices.

Things are looking brighter downtown with these innovations, but the old sector is not out of the woods yet. Problems remain, such as inadequate parking and a lack of diversified businesses, but the fact that there is a joint effort by political and civic leaders toward continued improvement is in itself encouraging.

Now it's 1910 and there are automobiles besides trolleys and horse-drawn vehicles. The Wallace Company has doubled its size in center background and the Orpheum movie theater has taken over the Ellis House building at left center.

The date of this picture is September 26, 1922, same corner. The autos are more numerous, the streetcars are bigger, and the Orpheum has become the Strand Theater.

State Street shops were well lighted during this afternoon rainstorm in the summer of 1936. Buses were by now rapidly replacing the electric cars, mainly because of the increase in automotive traffic. Lots of other changes can be seen from this same corner.

The State Street-Broadway corner today shows principally automobiles, although the Capital District Transportation Authority does have buses running on schedule. The Woolworth store at left, on the North Broadway corner, replaced the Vendome Hotel by 1938. There is not as much pedestrian traffic downtown because Schenectady, like most cities today, must share them with suburban malls.

## The Grade Crossings

Perhaps at no other time in Schenectady's long history had there been such an ambitious and time-consuming construction project as the raising of the railroad tracks through the city at the outset of the twentieth century. It was a long time in coming, with frequent mishaps, inconvenience and persistent urging by the citizenry, so there was widespread jubilation over its completion late in 1907.

Ever since a railroad station had been built downtown in 1836 to accommodate passengers of the early railroads—notably the Mohawk and Hudson, Saratoga and Schenectady, and Utica and Schenectady railroads—there was the problem and hazard of having to contend with grade level crossings. Naturally, it only worsened as the railroads got bigger and the population increased through the years.

It was when a young woman was killed on July 31, 1901 that public indignation finally prompted the railroads and city council to make definite arrangements to build overhead crossings. Miss Clytie C. Curtis, a pretty young General Electric employee, was riding her bicycle back to the plant after a midday meal uptown and tried to make the crossing ahead of a fast oncoming mail train. Her death was the eighth fatality at the State Street crossing alone since 1897.

The major costs of the track-raising project were borne by the New York Central and the Delaware & Hudson railroads, with a partial outlay by the city. D. D. Streeter & Company of Chicago was hired as general contractor and work started in the spring of 1903.

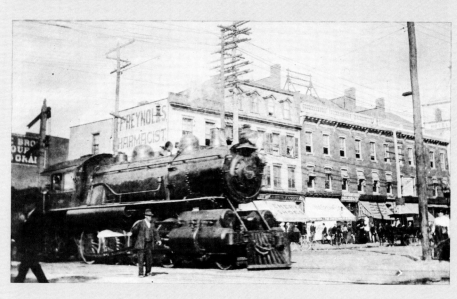

*A twelve-passenger horsecar trundles over the State Street railroad crossing in 1886.*

*By 1895, traffic over the railroad crossing had increased, and now included electric streetcars. The flagman's shanty is at right.*

*It was not unusual in the days of grade crossings for a train to hold up street traffic for as much as ten minutes—not to mention the hazard it presented.*

*Work is shown in progress on construction of the State Street overpass in 1905. Trolleys and other street traffic passed below the temporary trestles.*

*The State Street bridge as it looks now, eighty years after the raised tracks changed life in Schenectady for the better.*

It was calculated to be a five-year job, which was close to the actual time required. No wonder crowds of onlookers showed up daily to watch the procedure, so much was involved that demanded absolute and accurate timing on the part of engineers, architects and workers. Overhead crossings had to be built at thirteen locations throughout Schenectady and while the tracks were being raised, inches at a time, it was imperative that all traffic proceed with minimal delay. Thus, while the tracks were being raised on State Street above temporary wood trestles, electric streetcars and other traffic passed underneath through a veritable gully that had been scooped out before the trestle work began.

## The Hotel Corner

On the east corner of today's North Broadway and State Street once stood a hotel which, when opened in 1850, was considered part of Schenectady's "growing uptown business district." It was named the Eagle Hotel, a three-story brick structure that boasted "forty rooms, clean linen every day, and toilet facilities on each floor." Not bad for an inn of that period. When news reached Schenectady of the Appomattox surrender on April 9, 1865, ending the Civil War, the *Schenectady Daily Union* reported that "the biggest American flag ever seen in this city flew from the roof pole of the Eagle Hotel."

Between then and 1938 there was a succession of hotels, with new names but the same building, until a Woolworth five-and-dime took over the corner. There was the Carley House, the Barhydt House, the Hotel Vendome and the New Vendome, each being quite successful as the east end of the city's downtown expanded with the times. The corner not only was convenient to shopping but to the railroad station as well, only a block away.

*This was the Carley House shortly after it had taken over from the Eagle Hotel in 1875. That section of State Street was still unpaved but was strewn lightly with crushed stone. The alleyway at center led to the horse barns in the rear. Old North Centre Street, now North Broadway, is at left.*

*The same building (center background) was undergoing alterations, including a new clock tower, when this picture was made of a July 4, 1893, parade. When completed, the hotel reopened as the Barhydt House. Note the grade-level railroad crossing in foreground and the early two-truck streetcar in the background.*

*A view from an old tintype shows the Barhydt when it was newly opened, with its conspicuous clock tower, later in 1893. The church steeple in background, right of center, is the First Methodist Church at State and Lafayette streets.*

*The Hotel Vendome, shown here about 1900, assumed operations in the same building after 1897 so the Barhydt was short-lived. Schenectady's business and population were booming and now the east section of downtown was keeping up with the times—even a well-paved street and electric street lights.*

*The Vendome went out of business in 1936 and in its place was built the F. W. Woolworth Company store, which opened in 1938 and is still doing business at the corner once monopolized by hotels.*

*Patrolman Matthew McGinnis was a member of the traffic squad of the Schenectady Police Department when this picture was made in the early 1900s. In those days, most patrolling was done on foot or horseback but motorcycles were on the horizon. McGinnis, known as "Matt" to most everyone, was a popular officer on the beat and—as is evident in this picture—with pets as well. This was in front of the old city hall/police station on Jay Street as McGinnis was about to begin his rounds.*

*A police radio car checks traffic in the summer of 1941 at the intersection of Rice Road (foreground) and Washington Avenue and Erie Boulevard (background). By now, the traffic division needed patrol cars in all sections of the city, using radio communication with police headquarters to keep abreast of any and all emergencies.*

*Patrolman Gil Bisner stands beside his radio car 102 checking his clipboard data on the traffic situation before moving to another assignment. This is the same vantage point as shown in the 1941 photograph, certainly much changed since construction of Interstate 890 and the exit ramps.*

Among the earliest photographs made in Schenectady is this picture of Clute & Reagles implement shops about 1865. Actually fronting on Barrett Street, the shop buildings extended along State Street to Lafayette Street, shown at right in the photograph. Operated for many years by Peter I. Clute and James Reagles, the firm made agricultural implements and wheelbarrows. There were few homes in the vicinity at the time. Most existing buildings were inns, liveries or smithies.

The corner of State and Lafayette streets as it looks today.

## The Trolley Waiting Room

No matter what its official name was, when the Schenectady Railway Company Terminal opened in October 1913, everyone who rode the electric cars then and thereafter usually called it the "waiting room."

The gray blockstone building was erected at 512 State Street, one door in from the corner of State and Lafayette streets, and it soon became the focus of great activity in the downtown section of Schenectady. Large groups of people waited inside the cavernous structure as well as on the sidewalks all times of the day and night, the cars always stopping at the terminal with usual punctuality. Not only the urban cars, but the interurbans to neighboring cities (Albany, Troy, Amsterdam, Ballston Spa and Saratoga Springs) carried many passengers in those days before the automobile became a family commodity.

The waiting room, however, became a liability when the trolley company began to turn to motorized service in the early 1930s and passengers found it more convenient to board buses at other downtown street corners. Although it continued as a terminal for interurban bus service, the building fell into disuse and became an empty shell of its former splendor.

The property was sold to private interests in 1948 and two years later was converted to a four-story office building. Various businesses have occupied the ground floor over the years and people still stand on that corner. More likely as not, few of them are aware that this was once "the best place to catch the cars."

*The trolley waiting room in February 1948, when people were waiting for buses, not trolley cars. The terminal was sold that year and converted into an office building.*

*As the site looks today, corner of State and Lafayette streets in downtown Schenectady. St. Joseph's Catholic Church steeple is directly behind the four-story building that once was the trolley terminal.*

This impressive gray stone residence was once the home and office of Dr. Harmon Swits, a Schenectady physician of the mid-nineteenth century. It was built on that section of State Street east of the canal and railroad when housing was still sparse there, intermingled with inns and liveries. At first, the house number was 218 but changed to 430 State Street when addresses were upgraded on State and Union streets in 1886 for the first time since the early part of that century.

The property was purchased in 1916 by Charles W. Carl, owner of the Carl Company, which had been leasing a store since 1906 on lower State Street two doors below the canal bridge. The new Carl Company store opened in 1917 and was enlarged by more than half in 1925 on adjoining property to the west. Later to become known simply as ''Carl's,'' the department store has been one of Schenectady's best known and patronized stores in the downtown shopping area through more than eighty years. It also has located in four suburban shopping malls in the capital district.

This rooftop picture was made in the 1890s,
looking down on State Street from Jay Street
west toward the Broadway corner in the
center background. A parade is in progress,
separated in the right background by a
crossing freight train. Note the abundance
of utilities wires.

The same vantage point in 1936 from a print supplied by Glen P. Dalton, a former Schenectadian now living in Prospect Harbor, Maine. The Jay Street corner is at lower right, the Broadway corner at upper left. The trolley cars are still in operation.

As it looks today. Sidewalks are widened with irregular rest areas, the streetcars are long gone, and building facades have been brightened.

## A Popular Corner

The west corner of Jay and State streets has undergone periodic changes throughout the last century, beginning with construction in 1870 of a three-story brick building to be known as Union Hall. It replaced two small dwellings that had been built probably in the 1840s when that section of town was considered the vanguard of "uptown." Union Hall had a large theater auditorium on the second floor where stage shows, including the popular minstrel shows of that day, were performed.

In 1933, the old hall was pulled down and in its place was erected a modern, art deco two-story building for S. S. Kresge Company. By 1978, three years after Kresge's vacated the premises, a glass-roofed structure took over sites of three former stores—Kresge's, W. T. Grant, and the Wallace Company. The facades of the latter two buildings were retained for offices in this new building called Center City. [Featured within is a large skating arena for public and professional use.]

*All the fancy rigs in town were out for this grand inspection parade in the fall of 1903 in honor of the recently organized permanent fire department in Schenectady.*

*Fire Chief Henry Yates is seated in the one-horse buggy, center, leading his men from Jay Street in the center background. On that corner stood the majestic Union Hall, a*

*four-story brick building erected by 1870 as the city's first legitimate theater. A large stage and auditorium on the second floor provided live entertainment.*

The Union Hall block was removed in 1931 and in its place at State and Jay streets was built an S. S. Kresge store, which had just closed operations when this picture was made in 1973.

In the late 1970s, a major restoration project was undertaken at Jay and State streets. The S. S. Kresge store was replaced by a modern recreational facility called Center City, featuring ice skating, shows and offices. The facade of the former Wallace Company department store, left of center, was restored to its nineteenth century grandeur. Jay Street is at right.

Jay Street looks barely wide enough to handle this exodus from a matinee stage performance at the Van Curler Opera House on August 10, 1908. The theater's entrance is in the center background, on the corner of Franklin Street. The Second Reformed Church in the far left background would be removed in another year to make way for the federal building and post office.

Jay Street, often called Schenectady's "biggest little street," has had the reputation of being a busy mercantile strip despite its narrowness. The above view, made about 1900, shows little trouble with traffic in those days, but it became an increasing problem by the 1930s.

In 1984, Jay Street was closed to vehicular traffic and developed as a pedestrian shopping mall. It's the scene of frequent food fairs, sidewalk sales and outdoor dining.
Courtesy of John Papp

Tim Coakley and his jazz quartet entertain shoppers on the Jay Street mall near the Franklin Street side.

This was Liberty Street about 1870, looking westward over the canal bridge. The imposing residence of Charles Ellis, organizer of the Schenectady Locomotive Works in 1851, is barely visible through the trees at right center beyond the bridge. Isaac Bancker's smithy is in the far left background and Beal & Van Brunt's granary is in the right foreground. Streets are cobblestone with flagstone walks at intersections and gas lights at either end of the bridge. Wall Street leads to the left.

The same view in 1925, but the surroundings have altered. The old canal bed had recently been converted to Erie Boulevard and the Ellis house seems desolate in its setting. The Crown Hotel is in the left foreground at the Wall Street corner, the American Express offices in the building at right. Liberty Street ended at Ferry Street in the far center background.

*Not too different in 1950. Heffner's Grill is in the building at right, now known as the CIO Hall. The Ellis house is behind shade trees, and Liberty Street now extends west to Church Street.*

*But what a difference today! The old union hall was demolished in 1955 and the Crown Hotel met the same fate in 1971 when the station plaza was cleared for public parking. The Erie and State theaters once in the left center are gone, as is the Ellis house at right center where a Burger King restaurant now stands.*

The railroad station plaza at Wall and Liberty Streets in downtown Schenectady had been the site of presidential whistlestops for nearly a century before candidates forsook the railroad tours for jet planes and motorcades in the 1960s. Above, candidate Dwight D. Eisenhower makes a campaign speech in Schenectady on October 23, 1952, from a podium on the passenger platform overlooking the huge throng in the plaza below. The train station at left, fourth in the city's history, was opened in 1908.

The closing of the station by New York Central in 1970 and the removal of trackage on the west side prompted a vast change in that sector. Wall Street to the right was obliterated to augment a large parking area. Erie Boulevard is in the right background. Amtrak built a small station and waiting room at left. The Cushing Building, formerly the lower section of the Edison Hotel, is in the center background. The old railroad station once stood approximately in the center of this photograph.

*It was first called Crescent Park when developed at the east end of State Street above Lafayette Street in 1857, then termed a "delightful resting spot at the edge of the city." The above view is about 1880, showing the park at center as it divided State Street at the intersection of Lafayette Street. Once again, the familiar cobblestone streets, flagstone crosswalks, gas lamps and now-outdated buildings.*

*Renamed Veterans Park after the Korean War to honor veterans of all wars, the site is still well-maintained and restful for passersby. Some old-timers persist in calling it Crescent Park, recounting the pleasant times they spent there in days gone by.*

*Downtown Schenectady as it looks eastward from over the Mohawk River. Part of the Binnekill is at lower left, the community college at lower right. The State Street shopping district extends upward to the left of center. Courtesy of John Papp and Sid Brown*

*The south side of State Street between Lafayette and Clinton streets looked like this in 1910. The Schenectady Savings Bank, corner of Clinton and State, is shown at right while the new Foster Hotel is at left.*

*This present-day view looks eastward up State Street with Clinton Street at right. The Schenectady Savings Bank, now Northeast Savings, has been remodeled several times since it first occupied that corner in 1905. The former Foster Hotel was renovated recently into an apartment building.*

41

*A good view of the city of Schenectady could be had from the relative wilderness of the summit, as shown in this print from a glass negative made in 1889. The Edison Hotel, in the far center background, was then being constructed. Summit Avenue, developed along the top slope of the summit, still affords a fascinating glimpse of the valley below—provided one can look over rooftops.*

*This was a full-dress police funeral procession for Patrolman James A. Mynderse up Summit Avenue to the First English Lutheran Church on April 4, 1900. The officer died a hero's death while saving the life of a woman pedestrian at the grade-level railroad crossing on State Street. The newly built state armory is in the background.*

# The Summit

Once part of what was called the Bowery Woods (after the Dutch "bouwer" for woods) during most of the 19th century, Summit Avenue was developed in the early 1800s as housing spread farther up the hill above Veeder Avenue. Among the first to be laid out in the area of the Ramsay, Veeder, and Paige lots on the hill was Summit Avenue, appropriately called because it was along the site of picnickers, strollers and lovers who chose the Bowery Woods as a rendezvous for its beauty and enchantment.

Not only did it have numerous pathways through wooded areas of the rising slope, but also "lookout stations" along its summit where people could sit and enjoy an incredibly beautiful scene of the city below and the Mohawk Valley in the distance. Hues of the lower hills of Rotterdam and Glenville changed from morning to night with the slanting rays of the rising and setting sun.

Mostly two-family homes were built on Summit Avenue, at once a sought-after residential section because of its attractiveness and proximity to downtown Schenectady. It has remained a neighborhood of homes, although many changes have taken place around it. The old state armory down at the northern end has long disappeared, as has the Albany Street Theater (formerly the Empire) on the Germania Avenue corner. The fourteen-story Summit Towers rose above the northeast corner in the 1970s, its parking area decimating the ancient Henry Ramsay residence, which was the first dwelling on the hill. The former First English Lutheran Church midway up the east side is now the congregation of Refreshing Spring Church of God in Christ.

It is said that Arent Van Curler, leader of the Dutch founders of Schenectady in 1661, stood on the summit as early as 1642 on his way back to Fort Orange (Albany) and, looking over the valley below, declared it the "schoonst" (most beautiful) sight "the eyes of man have ever beheld."

*Summit Avenue as it looked in the spring of 1945, the vacated armory still down at the end and the historic Henry Ramsay residence at top right.*

*The same view as it looks today. Summit Towers, a senior housing project, is at right and Pulaski Plaza, which replaced the armory building, is at far center just across Albany Street.*

*Rows of simple but staid brick and wood homes lined both sides of Hamilton Street hill in this photograph of the 1880s, looking down toward old South Centre Street which became Broadway after 1910. John Wiederhold's woolen goods factory is in the center background. Originally, residents referred to this incline as Paige Hill because much of the property on the summit was owned by Alonzo W. Paige in the mid-1800s, but by the twentieth century it became Hamilton Hill.*

*Now the street is wider and paved with macadam instead of cobblestone. The Wiederhold building is still intact but has long since been used for purposes other than making ladies' garments, blankets and uniforms. Clinton Street at right was continued through to the left where it connects with Broadway near the Ten Eyck Apartments. All the houses at left are now gone, part of them razed to make way for the Schonowe Apartments in 1937 and the rest when the Clinton Street extension was built in 1961.*

# Early Almshouses

Taking care of the needy was a public responsibility recognized early in Schenectady after its chartering as a city in 1798. There were societies of the poor and countless church groups that had looked after the indigent in the community, but early in the 1800s a city almshouse and farm was developed on the high summit that today is known as Hamilton Hill.

Commonly referred to as "the poorhouse," this operation was taken over by the Schenectady County government in 1826 pursuant to a new state law that authorized the establishment of an almshouse in several counties of the state, Schenectady included. The county almshouse officially opened August 1, 1826, for the reception of county poor from the city and five townships of the county. Henry Clute, the first county "poorhouse keeper," was authorized to ensure maintenance and clothing of the inmates for sixty cents per week, the keeper being allowed the products of the farm and use of the buildings, and whatever labor he could obtain from able-bodied paupers.

The first almshouse and farm was quite a spread, but then, so was that portion of Schenectady in those earlier days. On the grounds were a long two-story wood building used as a men's dormitory, a second two-story building for women, and a good-sized brick building for the keeper's residence, offices and an infirmary. A large barn was at the rear and gardens were to the east.

*(Top photo)*
*The first Schenectady "poorhouse" was this group of three buildings constructed in the early 1800s on a section of open land on a summit east of the city which today is called Hamilton Hill.*

*(Middle photo)*
*Here is a picture of the former almshouse complex, at the corner of Craig Street (foreground) and Emmett Street (left), about 1900. Houses were being built in that area, now rapidly being developed.*

This is the same corner of Craig and Emmett streets, showing the St. Columba's Roman Catholic Church, built there in 1907 on the site of the almshouse. This church, abandoned in 1974 when the congregation merged with that of the Sacred Heart, was used as a community hall before it was demolished.

By 1880, development was under way in that area. One big project was the fairgrounds, established by the county not far east of the almshouse. It was used for a variety of events—agricultural shows, wagon-pulling contests, bike races, horse races and circuses—until it became apparent by the 1890s that the growth of the city was such that the spacious fairgrounds had to go. A state act was passed in 1900, authorizing Schenectady County to sell its poorhouse farm and buildings, the fairgrounds and its buildings and to lay out streets in the area for house construction. The sale of the land made it possible to erect a much-needed new almshouse.

This was done in 1901 as three brick buildings, interconnected by enclosed corridors, were built on the former poorhouse farm plot, bounded by Emmett Street, Brandywine Avenue, Duane Avenue and Steuben Street. Houses sprang up all around it in the new developments, and most of those homes are there today.

Changes in that area came in 1935 when the county built a new county home and farm out on Hetcheltown Road in Glenville. The newly formed Schenectady Museum took over the Steuben Street facilities, later demolishing a rear brick building. In 1966, soon after the museum left the hill premises to move into its new quarters on Terrace Place, the old almshouse was replaced on that block by the Martin Luther King Jr. Elementary School.

*(Top photo)*
*A 1937 view of the county home built in 1901 off Steuben Street to replace the original almshouse in that neighborhood. At this time it was being used by the Schenectady Museum because a new and larger county home known as Glendale had been erected in Glenville.*

*(Middle photo)*
*Now the Martin Luther King, Jr. Elementary School, built in 1966, occupies that block bounded by Steuben Street, Emmet Street, McClyman Street, and Duane Avenue.*

*On spacious grounds amid rolling hills of Glenville farm country, the Glendale Home opened in 1935 as a modern county home for indigent and/or aged citizens of Schenectady County. For many years, a county-operated farm was maintained on the premises, partially with help of able-bodied residents of the home, but it eventually was discontinued. Located on Hetcheltown Road, just north of Glenridge Road, Glendale Home now boasts a large infirmary, shown under construction in this aerial view of November 1977.*

This is a southerly view of South Centre Street at the junction of Liberty Street, which is in the foreground, left to right. The picture is from pre-World War I days, probably about 1912, when there were many commercial establishments on that narrow thoroughfare. State Street is in the far center background.

*The same vantage point as it is today, except that South Centre Street is now North Broadway. Many of the old buildings were removed during the past decade to provide additional downtown parking.*

# In and Around the City

What is generally referred to now as "downtown Schenectady" is the area that encompassed the residential section a little more than a century ago. When President-elect Abraham Lincoln spoke briefly from the rear platform of his railroad coach to the thousands gathered alongside the grade level tracks on February 18, 1861, he could virtually see both ends of town—the foot of State Street at the banks of the Mohawk River on the western end and the head of State Street at the college terrace on the eastern end.

As previously stated, that all changed and drastically—after 1890 with the influx of immigrant families drawn to Schenectady largely because of Edison's machine works, which became the General Electric Company by 1892. Neighborhoods sprang up where orchards, vacant fields or wooded lots once existed. Suburban communities were developed just outside the fringes of the city limits, but so did the original city expand to its perimeters on all sides east of the river.

Houses were built everywhere, particularly where the Schenectady Railway Company extended its urban routes after 1900. Albany Street, State Street, Nott Terrace, Wendell Avenue, Eastern Avenue, McClellan Street, Van Vranken Avenue— they and connecting side streets were soon populated, and older folks scratched their heads in amazement.

The Schenectady Union-Star *was a Schenectady evening newspaper when two older dailies merged in 1911. The* Schenectady Evening Star, *which was founded in 1857, and the* Schenectady Daily Union, *founded in 1865, were no longer in competition when the* Union-Star *began operations in a Clinton Street building following the merger. However, a modern plant was constructed, as shown in the above picture made June 25, 1926, two days before the cornerstone ceremony. The print emulsion was damaged when water leaked into the cornerstone box, recovered when the building was demolished forty-five years later. At left, printers in the old* Union-Star *building are gawking out the windows at the construction work next door. The Morse Bowling Alley, 207-211 Clinton Street had previously occupied the site.*

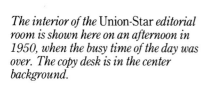

*As the new building looked when it was completed in 1927. The old building next door later was used by the United Scottish Organization and became known as the USO Hall.*

*The interior of the* Union-Star *editorial room is shown here on an afternoon in 1950, when the busy time of the day was over. The copy desk is in the center background.*

*The exterior of the* Union-Star *building in 1950. The newspaper was sold to Hearst Newspapers in 1969 and moved to Albany as the* Knickerbocker News-Union-Star. *However, the "Union-Star" part was soon dropped.*

*The vacated* Union-Star *building was demolished in April 1971 after it had been purchased by the former Schenectady Savings Bank (now Northeast Savings) for expansion purposes. The bank also bought and razed the old USO Hall in 1969. Today, the only vestige of the* Union-Star *days is the warehouse building at right, once used for newsprint storage.*

In the early 1890s, Clinton Street was one of the busier downtown thoroughfares in Schenectady, yet it was mainly residential. Here is a northerly view of Clinton Street of that period, looking from Hamilton Street toward Smith Street. A carbon arc streetlight hangs at top center, a former gaslight pole is on the corner at right, the houses are a mixture of brick and wood, a cistern cover is in the left foreground, and the street is paved with cobblestone.

The same vantage point as it looks today shows a tremendous change from the neighborhood atmosphere to one of openness as additional parking space was needed. Most houses along this part of Clinton Street were razed during the 1950s as parking lots were installed for use by theatergoers, bank patrons, shoppers and employees. Northeast Savings Bank is in the right center background at State Street, and Proctor's Theatre is at left. However, at least one thing was unchanged—the same brick house is at right.

The Salvation Army, whose Schenectady corps was organized in 1883, completed this citadel on Lafayette Street in 1909. St. Joseph's parochial school, the brick building partly seen at right, was a few doors north toward State Street. Both were demolished about the same time in 1974, the school having closed a few years before. However, the Salvation Army had already built a new edifice at the corner of Lafayette and Smith streets, nearly next door to the old one.

The present Salvation Army citadel, as viewed from Smith Street looking down Lafayette Street. This one is equipped with a gymnasium-auditorium and offices besides the hall used for religious services. On this corner was once located a general store run for many years by Andrew Torra and his son Frank.

Another Henry Tripp glass negative print of the 1880s shows the west corner of Veeder Avenue (left) and State Street. At that time, this area was near the fringe of Schenectady's urban section to the east. On the corner at left is Joseph Trentman's Park House. The confectionery store next door sold ice cream, then becoming a popular item in America.

The same corner, about 1920, as viewed from across Crescent Park. At right is the county courthouse, completed in 1915, and to its left the central fire station, which opened July 1, 1900. Courtesy of White Studio

By 1956, the Modern Diner had already
established long-time residency at the
Veeder-State corner and Veeder Avenue had
been made one-way for north traffic in
that block.

Now it's a new scene entirely. The county
office building on the corner opened in
1962, the county jail in the right
background was renovated only two years
ago and the entire avenue has more than
doubled in width.

## Yates Street

Yates Street is one of Schenectady's narrowest and shortest downtown streets, yet it represents a sizeable portion of the city's early history.

Developed soon after the American Revolution and named after Joseph C. Yates, first mayor of Schenectady and eighth governor of New York State, Yates Street soon became a distinguished residential area. In 1835 was built the Schenectady Lyceum and Academy, a private school for boys, which lasted until 1854 when public schools were established. Among its students was Chester A. Arthur, later to become a United States president, who also graduated from Union College in 1848.

Mostly brick homes were built along Yates Street, with side-entry stoops hugging the narrow sidewalks. With Liberty Street on the south end and Union Street on the north end, Yates Street was a natural traffic connector for vehicles of early days— wagons, carriages, sleighs and bicycles. Yet, it maintained a certain elegance until the 1940s. Thereafter, the demand for more parking in that area resulted in many houses being torn down.

Yates Street was never widened so it was not conducive to use by heavy modern traffic. Aside from a few commercial buildings on the street, it now serves primarily as a feeder connection to and from parking lots.

*Very few residences exist today on Yates Street as is apparent in this view from the same vantage point. Parking lots are on all sides.*

*Many of the houses, mostly brick, were still along Yates Street in the 1930s when this picture was made, looking north toward Union Street. The former Schenectady Lyceum once was located on the far right corner. Dr. Dayton L. Kathan's impressive home, built in 1901 and headquarters for the Schenectady Boy's Club since 1942, is in far left background.*

The corner of Yates Street is at left as we look eastward up Liberty Street in the 1880s. In the upper center is the steeple of the old Second Reformed Church, which was razed in 1908 to make way for a new post office at Jay and Liberty streets. The brick house at left was the parsonage of the First Baptist Church where young Chester A. Arthur lived with his family in the 1840s.

A much different area today, less tranquility and greater movement of people and vehicles. Some of the old homes remain but most, such as the former Arthur house at left, have been remodeled and converted into businesses.

59

The Schenectady Locomotive Works had earned the name "Big Shop" by the time this picture was made in the late 1870s. This was Fonda Street, at the end of which is a bridge over the Erie Canal at Nott Street. A gas street lamp is in front of the administration building at center. The works was started in 1848 and soon became one of the prime manufacturers of locomotive steam engines in this country.

After 1901, the works merged with several other locomotive builders and became known as the American Locomotive Company, generally referred to as Alco. The plant grew rapidly, expanding to the west or opposite side of the canal, even entering the auto and truck manufacturing business in 1905 for an eight-year period. Alco was busy during World War II building both locomotives and army tanks. This view, made in the winter of 1954 from the same vantage point as the earlier photograph, shows a later administration building soon to be razed. In 1955, the company was renamed Alco Products Incorporated because it had diversified and was manufacturing other products besides locomotives.

This is North Jay Street, once Fonda Street, and just beyond the raised railroad tracks is the vacant space where the locomotive works first began, now a parking lot for a Ramada Inn on Nott Street. The end of locomotive manufacturing in Schenectady, which actually ended several years before, was officially declared in 1968 when Alco's doors were closed. Since that time, General Electric has taken over many of Alco's factory buildings but a few others on Erie Boulevard are used by smaller corporations.

## The Old Armory Site

When the first state armory was erected in 1868 near the summit of the State Street hill, there were few houses in that vicinity. Crescent Park was in its development stage just below it, and open fields stretched upward beyond the eastern fringes of the hill.

When the thirty-sixth and thirty-seventh separate companies of the state guard left for service in the Spanish-American War in 1898, construction began on the second armory. By now, there was housing all about and trolley cars passed by the armory site on all sides and directions.

This second armory was a popular spot for sporting events and civic functions for nearly four decades. Even while the present state armory was functioning after 1937 on Washington Avenue, the "old drillshed" uptown was used for public events until its demolition in 1947.

What a change had overtaken that old armory site in eighty years! The area was heavily populated with housing, commercial buildings and road vehicles. Scarcely had the armory been leveled that summer when work was started to widen Armory Place between State and Albany streets.

In 1950, the Polish National Alliance completed development of the remaining portion of the armory lot into a picturesque park to be known as Pulaski Plaza, honoring the Polish general who died a hero's death in the American Revolution. A monument of Casimir Pulaski was unveiled in 1953.

*Schenectady's original state armory near the top of the State Street hill as it looked upon completion in 1868.*

*The second state armory, built upon the same site by 1899, is shown here about 1903 looking at its north entrance from the Nott Terrace side.*

*The armory as it was being torn down in the summer of 1947.*

*Dedication ceremonies were held in the summer of 1950 to mark the opening of Pulaski Plaza on the site of the old armory.*

*Pulaski Plaza and the Pulaski monument as it looks today. Summit Avenue is in the center background and Summit Towers in the left background.*

Several blocks of homes, most of them built in the 1870s and showing their age, were leveled in 1956 and 1957 just east of Schenectady's city hall block as a federal urban renewal project was started. Here, a weathered wood house at Terrace Place and Blaine Street is shown just before and after it was pulled down. These and several other streets were obliterated by the project.

For a time, the project was stalled by indecision over what was to be built in the leveled area. Here is the sidewalk corner of Johnson Street and Terrace Place in 1958, now overgrown with weeds, awaiting some kind of action.

Finally, a large Two Guys department store was constructed along the Lafayette Street end of the project, the remainder used for parking. The store closed four years ago and has since been taken over by General Electric for offices.

John B. Freudigman's bottling works at 727 State Street handled wholesale orders for all kinds of bottled lager and ale, but also admitted customers who wanted to drink on the premises. Two employees pose outside the premises at 727 State Street in the 1890s. Later, the firm moved to 1298 Albany Street where Freudigman operated a saloon.

A music store currently occupies the site at 727 State Street where Freudigman's works had been located.

Construction of St. Clare's Hospital in a hilly pinewoods section of McClellan Street was started in January 1948, the culmination of several years of planning and fundraising on behalf of the Catholic Diocese of Albany. Bishop Edmund Gibbons presided over the cornerstone ceremony on June 13 that year.

This is the main entrance to St. Clare's as it looks today. The original portion is the rounded section at left, toward McClellan Street, while the new addition is at right. On June 7, 1973, Bishop Edwin B. Broderick conducted another cornerstone ceremony, this time for the $14 million expansion, which more than doubled the size of the original facility.

Louis Hildebrandt was proprietor of a carriage inn at the top of the State Street hill in the latter half of the nineteenth century, serving as a stopover or resting point for weary stagecoach passengers on the old Albany Turnpike. He is shown above (man with white shirt, fifth from left) outside his establishment. The boy in the foreground stands beside an outdoor public water pump.

Today, the site of the Hildebrandt inn is occupied by the Schenectady Eagles Aerie 514, now 916 State Street, between Steuben and Martin streets. That location has continued in the hostelry tradition since the early part of this century as various restaurants have done business there.

Traffic on Schenectady's main street was still uncongested past the downtown section as evidenced in this mid-afternoon 1926 picture on State Street looking westward toward the hill to the shopping area. The car at left is on Steuben Street. Trolley tracks run down the center of the street.

There are no streetcars today on State Street but automobiles and trucks. This is the same view sixty-two years later. Steuben Street is still at left.

Civic excitement was widespread in 1900 when the decision was made to build a new and grand public high school up on Nott Terrace. The architect's preliminary drawing, shown above, added to the anticipation. It was altered considerably in the final draft in order to cut costs.

The cornerstone laying ceremony, shown here, took place on June 18, 1902— although 1903 was inscribed on the stone. Union Street is in background, beyond the corner house.

By 1909, it was found that the north building, or original structure, was inadequate for the rapidly growing city, so a second and adjoining facility called the south building was built in 1911. It was called Schenectady High School until the fall of 1931, when it became Nott Terrace High School. That was the year Mont Pleasant High School opened.

A westward view down Eastern Avenue shows the site on Nott Terrace where the high school once stood. The south building was razed in 1962 for the widening of Liberty Street, while the north building was torn down in 1974 and replaced on that site by a restaurant. The old high school was no longer needed after 1956 when Linton High opened.

*Andrew Schinnerer, a German immigrant, set up a brewery in the late 1850s at the southwest corner of Union and Centre streets which grew to be among the busiest locally. Known as the Centre Street Brewery, a likeness shown here from an 1866 city directory advertisement, it ceased operation in the late 1870s.*

*The brewery building was used as a warehouse in later years, as shown in this photograph of about 1930. The letters that spell "BREWERY" can be seen on the side of the brick facade at center.*

*The old brewery site, now North Broadway and Union Street, has been occupied for several years by the Acme Press, which recently modernized its plant. During the renovation, workmen uncovered several of the brick-lined storage rooms used by the Centre Street Brewery and found some artifacts of a bygone era.*

Morning shadows are cast across the cobblestone pavement of South Centre Street in this photograph of about 1906. Later to be renamed Broadway, this section of the city's Fifth Ward had become heavily populated with low- to middle-income housing on both sides of that well-used roadway. This is a northerly view toward State Street. Frederick Stein's Cafe at right was on the corner of Veeder Avenue. The trolley cars in the center background made the run southward up to the end of Broadway or Campbell Avenue in Bellevue.

Housing in that area is at a minimum today and much changed, as seen here, from eighty years ago. Except for the municipal housing projects, Broadway consists mainly of businesses and warehousing. A self-service gasoline station at right is located on the former site of Stein's Cafe. The lower portion of Veeder Avenue has been closed.

P. S. and R. J. Lynch were wagon makers who operated a wagon shop and smithy at 432 South Centre Street from 1896 until 1922. Shown here is the entrance to the Lynch Brothers Shop about 1900, with Patrick's brick home at left.

The Lynch brothers (center, with hammers over their right shoulders) pose outside the shop with their crew of blacksmiths and wagon repairmen.

When Centre Street became Broadway shortly after the turn of the century, the wagon shop's address became 318 Broadway. Now located at that site is the Tri-City Saw & Tool Company. The former brick house is still next door.

In 1949, construction of a low-income housing project by the Municipal Housing Authority in Schenectady was well in progress as shown here. It was located at the end of Van Vranken Avenue and, because it was just north of Yates School on Salina Street, was named Yates Village. When fully completed and dedicated the following year, it was filled to capacity in short order.

Yates Village has served the public well in the interim. It underwent extensive remodeling and repairs in 1984 and 1985, improving playgrounds and exterior design as well as the interior of the apartments. Photograph by Sid Brown, courtesy of Schenectady Gazette

*The lower end of Van Vranken Avenue extension, next to the community of Craig, looked like this in 1890. The unpaved road was partially cut out of the hillside. The Erie Canal and the Mohawk River were to the right.*

*As this same place looks today. The canal is long gone, the paved road is wider, and the traffic a mite heavier and faster.*

The McClellan Street car barn for the
trolleys of the Schenectady Railway
Company, shown here in the 1920s, opened
in 1903, four years after the Fuller Street
car barn began operation.

After the streetcars were phased out in the
summer of 1946, the barns were used
strictly for buses. The above view of the front
of the McClellan Streen barn was made
in 1950.

The Fuller Street facility was demolished
and replaced by a union hall in the 1960s,
but the one at McClellan Street and Eastern
Parkway fared better. It became a
department store for a few years, but on
March 23, 1976, the grand opening for a
new Price Chopper market presaged a busy
future for the old car barn.

The exterior of the McClellan Street
building as it looks today.

Joseph Schreck was among many German immigrants who came to Schenectady at the turn of this century and settled on Albany Street. Not only was he an excellent carpenter, builder and construction contractor, but he also became the proprietor of a boarding house and recreation hall at his address, 1118 Albany Street. Here, his establishment is shown in 1917 where he had the Owl Hotel, his office as a contractor, and Schreck's Hall—complete with bar, dining room, and bowling alley.

*The premises look quite the same today— minus, of course, all the business operations, because it is now for apartment dwellers only.*

# Woodlawn...How It's Grown!

Before the 1920s, the region above the city line at Fehr Avenue was largely rural—at least the houses were generally scattered. Interurban trolleys zipped through the countryside along Route 5 but upper Albany Street was unpaved and sparsely settled.

But the area began to change after World War I. More streets were developed and houses built along them. Soon there was public agitation toward annexation by the city so that residents and future home owners would have the benefits of sewers, fire hydrants, paving, trash collection and those other modern refinements enjoyed by city dwellers. The

city council approved the annexation in 1922 and it became effective the next year.

The city line was moved eastward on State Street out near the Balltown Road intersection and Woodlawn became the city's Fourteenth Ward. The whole area became widely settled by the late 1930s and State Street was turned into a commercial strip.

Although the Woodlawn boundary should begin at Fehr Avenue, site of the original city limits, most people living east of Brandywine Avenue say they are from Woodlawn. And why not? It has always been a pleasant community.

This was the pavilion of the old Brandywine Park on upper Albany Street, which started out in the 1880s as a recreation field but became a bona fide amusement park in 1896 when the Schenectady Railway Company purchased and redeveloped the site. Heavyweight boxing champ Jack Dempsey fought an exhibition match here in 1923 a month before his celebrated fight with Luis Angel Firpo. The park hosted dances, group outings, track events and family picnics well into the 1920s before it fell into disuse.

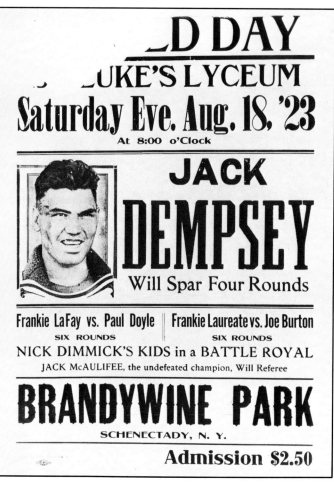

_D DAY

_ LUKE'S LYCEUM

Saturday Eve. Aug. 18, '23

At 8:00 o'Clock

JACK

DEMPSEY

Will Spar Four Rounds

Frankie LaFay vs. Paul Doyle | Frankie Laureate vs. Joe Burton

SIX ROUNDS | SIX ROUNDS

NICK DIMMICK'S KIDS in a BATTLE ROYAL

JACK McAULIFEE, the undefeated champion, Will Referee

BRANDYWINE PARK

SCHENECTADY, N. Y.

Admission $2.50

The park site was taken over by St. Luke's Roman Catholic Church in the 1930s. The old pavilion was enclosed and the interior converted to a community hall for church social functions. Since its dedication September 18, 1955, St. Luke's School has occupied the spacious lot. The school is shown at right, Albany Street at left.

*A man and his young daughter are out for a buggy ride in this 1911 photograph made on upper Albany Street, then sparsely settled with dirt roads everywhere.*

*This same spot, now 3002 Albany Street, has been occupied since 1919 by Fire Station No. 10, serving the Woodlawn area, which has become heavily populated with both homes and businesses.*

The annual Soap Box Derby drew hundreds of spectators to the Fehr Avenue hillside each summer in Schenectady during the late 1930s and throughout the 1940s. The above action shows a view from State Street during the derby trials in the late 1940s.

Fehr Avenue today. It's a well-used thoroughfare for people going to Central Park or upper Union Street.

*Two derby contestants on the ramp at the top of the hill get set for the "go" sign.*

This was upper State Street in the 1880s, but officially called East Avenue, looking west from Brandywine Avenue. There was no paving, just rutted (and often muddy) dirt, even though housing was beginning to spread eastward from Nott Terrace. Note the horsecar in the far center background, which operated from Washington Avenue up to the horsecar barn on South Brandywine Avenue.

Today, the same view shows a still spacious roadway—but long since paved with macadam and bordered by homes and businesses that stretch all the way to Albany, some fifteen miles distant.

Woodlawn was a suburb of Schenectady when this photograph was made about 1915 on the Albany-Schenectady Road (Route 5) looking east toward Schenectady. Yale Street is at left, where it crossed the tracks of the Schenectady Railway Company, on which the Albany interurban cars ran on regular schedule. Woodlawn became the Fourteenth Ward when annexed to the city in 1923.

The same vantage point as it looks today. The trolley tracks were removed by the mid-1930s when buses replaced the electric cars, and shortly thereafter Route 5 was doubled in size. As can be seen in comparing the two photos, many of the same buildings remain yet today.

The Temple Gates of Heaven synagogue decided early in the 1950s to move from Parkwood Boulevard and Rugby Road into more spacious quarters, a new edifice to be built at Eastern Parkway and Ashmore Avenue. Here, in September 1954, is a picture of the groundbreaking ceremony held just prior to construction. Alexander Diamond, a Schenectady attorney, is shown at left addressing the assemblage. Behind him (arms folded) is then Mayor Archibald C. Wemple.

# Upper Union Street

In old photographic albums housed in the City History Center are several that fit into the category of Upper Union Street, considered that area of Union Street which stretches from Brandywine Avenue up to the city line above Van Antwerp Road. In captions accompanying many of those views, the late city historian William B. Efner often used the terms "these fine homes" or "fine residential community."

Who could blame him? The upper Union Street section still has that touch of class, retaining residential beauty on its tree-shaded side streets while permitting commercial zoning on the eastern end of the main street. Many of the stately homes between Union and Lakewood avenues have long since been converted into professional laboratories and offices, so much so that it's been referred to as "Doctor's Row." East past Lakewood, there are mainly businesses on both sides, the kinds of stores and boutiques shoppers seek out in the suburban malls. The Troy Savings Bank is among the newer businesses to locate there.

The Upper Union Street Merchants Association has a long-standing record of organization and promotion, its primary aim being to impress upon people that in-town shopping is not out of fashion. The variety of stores in the area today, a far cry from fifty years ago, has made the association's job much easier.

# New on the block...

Among the new businesses on upper Union Street is the Schenectady office of The Troy Savings Bank, located at 1626 Union Street which years ago was the site of the residence of Mrs. Emma Way and, later, of the Union 5 & 10 store.

In 1988, Troy Savings was celebrating two anniversaries—on April 25, the first year of its Schenectady office; and on August 30, the 165th year of its founding. There are now seven branch offices besides the main bank in Troy; Schenectady, East Greenbush, Whitehall, Clifton Park, Glens Falls, Watervliet, and Hudson Valley Plaza.

It may be relatively a "new kid on the block" at upper Union Street, but The Troy Savings Bank is the oldest state-chartered savings bank in New York State. It's interesting to note that at the close of its first day's business on August 30, 1823, the books showed $359 had been deposited in the ten accounts opened. Some change from today, as total assets for Troy Savings as of December 31, 1987, were more than $478 million.

*The Union 5 & 10 store at 1626 Union Street, built in February 1952, is now the location of The Troy Savings Bank's Schenectady office.*

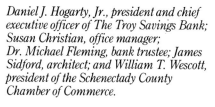

*This was the opening of Troy Savings' Schenectady office on April 25, 1987. At the tape-cutting ceremony, from left are Michael J. Cahill, president of Duncan & Cahill, contractor; Charles and Millie Eisenberg, owners of the former Union 5 & 10; Congressman Samuel S. Stratton, Schenectady Mayor Karen B. Johnson;*

*Daniel J. Hogarty, Jr., president and chief executive officer of The Troy Savings Bank; Susan Christian, office manager; Dr. Michael Fleming, bank trustee; James Sidford, architect; and William T. Wescott, president of the Schenectady County Chamber of Commerce.*

*The interior of the Schenectady office of The Troy Savings Bank has individual offices, in addition to a teller's counter where private banking can be transacted.*

At the city line on upper Union Street, there was an obvious demarcation between urban and suburban life when this picture was made about 1930. Houses were sparse on either side beyond this point, then considered the start of Troy Road on Route 7. The interurban trolleys of the Schenectady Railway Company went along the tracks at right, beside the two-lane macadam road. The Richfield Oil gasoline station, managed by Clifton F. Williams, is at left on the corner of Van Antwerp Road. In another five years, this scene changed considerably as the tracks were removed and the highway widened.

Today, this same area is a bustling section of upper Union Street but continues far past the Van Antwerp Road corner. The four-lane Route 7 leading eastward to Latham and Troy no longer is "countrified." Now, homes and businesses have filled in those wide, open spaces.

Construction of St. Stephen's Episcopal Church was well under way in the summer of 1949, as shown in this view from The Plaza near Baker Avenue. Much of the stone came from the old state armory at State and Albany Streets, which had been demolished in 1947.

This was the unfinished sanctuary of St. Stephen's, also the summer of 1949.

As it looks today, fitting in comfortably with its sedate surroundings.

The house shown here was among the first to be built on Duryee Avenue, a name changed later to Bedford Road. This was about 1904, when work had commenced on the Elmer Avenue School just down the block. Note the workman beside the horse-drawn wagon in right center, engaged in clearing rocks and stumps preparatory to installation of a paved street with curbing and sidewalks. Eastern Avenue was to the rear of the wagon, running left to right, where the electric cars of Schenectady Railway Company had just begun operation.

Now, eighty-four years later, that same house (center) is Number 904 Bedford Road, at the corner of Eastern Avenue. It still has the same lines—windows, roof, peaks, etc.—but the porches have been altered and the wood has been covered with aluminum siding. Other things have changed, too. The neighborhood rapidly became densely populated, although it remains a desirable residential area "only a stone's throw" from downtown Schenectady.

Mont Pleasant's Crane Street was a desolate, muddy track in the 1880s before massive housing development began only a few years after this photograph was made on a glass plate negative. The view is southeast toward the corner where Chrisler Avenue (left) enters Crane Street. It was over this section of Chrisler Avenue that the locomotive DeWitt Clinton pulled three coaches of passengers in 1831 from Albany to the top of Crane Street hill. Schenectady became the western terminus of the pioneering Mohawk & Hudson Railroad.

# It's Called Mont Pleasant

There are numerous scenic hills in Schenectady, those which overlook the city itself and the wooded ramparts of the Mohawk Valley just beyond. One of these certainly is the escarpment with the peaceful name of Mont Pleasant.

One old-time Schenectadian, reflecting on his early boyhood in that area, once wrote that in the late 1890s many folks actually walked up the long, steep Crane Street hill to reach a spot near the top called Sunset Hill—just to enjoy the beautiful view of the mountains of Rotterdam and Glenville. Sunset Street, long since filled with homes, is on that site.

It seems that Mont Pleasant was so named about 1890. At least that's when it first appeared in the Schenectady city directory under the suburban listing. Before that, it was listed as "Engine Hill and Mohawkville." This was the time of the beginning of widespread housing development on that hill and, just like neighboring Bellevue, it was annexed to the city of Schenectady in 1902. Mont Pleasant became the Ninth Ward.

Crane Street was named after Jonathan Crane, who about 1823 undertook a flax mill and factory that in time became a flourishing business known as the Mohawk Thread and Twine Company. Since his factories were at the end of present-day Crane Street and Altamont Avenue, the road leading from the mill to Engine Hill was called Crane Street. Crane's industry also influenced the naming of a small settlement between Curry Road and Crane Street—Mohawkville.

Mont Pleasant rapidly blossomed into a residential neighborhood as newly developed streets shunted off Crane Street and Chrisler Avenue, were soon filling up with new houses, both one-family and multiple-family dwellings. With all these families crowding into the area, the Third Avenue School was erected in 1893 to supplement the Mohawkville one-room schoolhouse at the opposite end of Crane Street, followed by Seward School at Congress and Fifth streets and McKinley School at Willett Street and Oakland Avenue in 1908, and Hamilton School in 1914. Still later, to replace outdated buildings, Pleasant Valley School was built in 1922 at Forest Road and Craig Street, and Mont Pleasant High School was added in 1931 at Forest Road and Norwood Avenue.

The opening of electric car service into Mont Pleasant by the Schenectady Railway Company on March 31, 1905—across the trolley bridge built over Pleasant Valley—generated even greater population growth. Today, many of these homes built at the turn of this century are still well-kept along Mont Pleasant's shaded neighborhood streets. Countless families of Polish, Hungarian and Italian extraction have remained there in the same houses first built by their immigrant forebears.

Crane Street has always been Mont Pleasant's main thoroughfare and, as such, has been the focus for merchants to set up shop. The Crane Street Merchants Association was organized many years ago and is still active in overseeing both the growth and quality of businesses in that shopping district.

If asked to define the boundaries of Mont Pleasant, one might be hard-pressed to be precise because none has been officially defined. However, it is generally known to include Crane and intersecting streets from Broadway to Altamont Avenue.

*The same view in 1917, with Chrisler
Avenue at left and Crane Street continuing
to the right toward Rotterdam. The trolley
tracks at right were installed when the
electric cars came to Mont Pleasant in
1905. The Odd Fellows Hall in center
background also was used for showing
motion pictures under the name of
Bijou Theatre.*

The horse watering trough at Chrisler and Crane was well used before the combustion engine took full control of transportation by the late 1930s. Here, in this photo made one early July morning in 1918, two milk deliverymen give their horsepower an aqua recharge at the cast-iron fount.

Today, Crane Street is filled with commercial establishments mainly between Francis Avenue and the Chrisler-Crane junction in the background. The IOOF Hall has since been replaced at that corner by a gasoline station and grocery store.

*A narrow humpback bridge over the New York Central Railroad tracks near the end of Crane Street became increasingly hazardous and troublesome to motorists by the beginning of the post-World War II era. As shown in this July 1957 photograph, its tight squeeze could not accommodate a bus and auto going in opposite directions, which necessitated the installation of a one-way traffic light system.*

*By the 1960s, a new and wider bridge was built to alleviate the problem of traffic tie-ups along upper Crane Street, caused mainly by the one-way waiting time at the old span. Both of these views, made thirty years apart, are from subsidiary tracks of the former New York Central Railroad (later Penn Central and now Amtrak) overpass looking west toward the city proper. This is just outside the Rotterdam town line near Altamont Avenue.*

Pleasant Valley was the name finally given a heavily wooded vale that for years before 1900 was called Cotton Factory Hollow because a man named Archibald Craig operated a cotton mill and factory off Craig Street, utilizing the dammed-up Sand Kill for power. It was a year-round playground for youngsters living in that vicinity. Left is a 1952 view from Broadway, which was the lower extremity of the valley, showing the curious structure known as the Klondike ramp that was built in the mid-1930s to replace a series of steps called the Klondike stairs leading down from Strong Street. The wooded area and narrow macadam road are at right.

Below, it was also 1952 when workmen began cutting timber and clearing the way for the planned state construction of Interstate 890 through Pleasant Valley. Wylie Street is in background.

An easterly view up the denuded Pleasant Valley in late 1952 toward the former Maqua Company plant in the center background shows grading work and the Sand Kill being submerged in culverts preparatory to construction of I-890, known as the Thruway spur. This is above the Craig Street viaduct and Wylie Street is at left.

Years went by before I-890 construction actually began, its opening taking place in 1968. This is a westerly view from Craig Street looking down the divided, multi-lane interstate toward the Cotton Factory Hollow Bridge, which replaced the Hulett Street trolley bridge in 1981.

Near the Broadway exit off I-890 can be seen part of the old Klondike ramp in right background. The Klondike, sometimes referred to as "Seven Heavens" because of its seven tiers, was razed in 1958 after it was deemed unsafe.

*Beckwith Pond, between Crane Street and Chrisler Avenue, was a popular spot for community fishing, swimming and skating for many years. It was part of the estate of Clarence A. Beckwith who, with his brother Charles D. Beckwith of New York City, operated a construction and real estate firm during the early part of this century. This is a 1930 view from atop a concrete wall abutment on Crane Street looking toward the Beckwith house at 800 Chrisler Avenue.*

*After the Beckwith estate was bequeathed to the Schenectady YMCA for a Mont Pleasant branch in 1952, the pond was used more widely under supervised conditions for youth recreation. Above, boys and girls are shown during ice skating races in the winter of 1952-53.*

*This is how the area looks today in this view made from the same concrete wall from Crane Street toward Chrisler Avenue. The pond was filled in, primarily as a safety precaution, a few years after the Mont Pleasant YMCA headquarters was established. At the same time, the old Beckwith house was demolished and replaced by a modern building, surrounded by a playground complete with swimming pool.*

A 1910 view from the porch of Alfred J. Kinns' store at 415 Francis Avenue in Mont Pleasant, looking north toward the trolley bridge from Hulett Street. Note the horse-driven wagon pulling out of Bridge Street at left and the electric car on the bridge just beyond it. The neighborhood was filling with homes but the street was still unpaved.

The Mont Pleasant end of the trolley bridge, constructed in 1903-04 and opened for service in 1905. This gave the Ninth Ward a closer tie with the main part of the city on the other side of Pleasant Valley. The bridge ceased to be used for trolleys after 1930 and shortly after was converted to automobile traffic.

Again, from the front of 415 Francis Avenue, only this time in 1987. The same two houses that were in the 1910 picture are still across the street at right. The new Cotton Factory Hollow Bridge in the center background replaced the former trolley bridge in 1981.

*The Thomas E. Wilson & Company, shown above at Hawthorne Street (right) and Ten Eyck Avenue (left), was a familiar fixture in that area from the time it opened in 1921 for the manufacture of sporting goods until its closing in 1955. The firm hired about 100 people, many of them women, to make and sew covers on baseballs and softballs. A year after its closing, the building became the Maqua Printing Company branch office and storage plant.*

*The United States Post Office constructed a distribution and sorting center on the premises of the old sporting goods factory, opening it on July 4, 1976. This is the same corner, Hawthorne Street at right, Ten Eyck at left.*

*Bellevue's Campbell Avenue, near Fifth Street, looked like this about 1915—a growing community, streetcar service and paved road.*

# The Hilltop Community

Bellevue was a part of the Town of Rotterdam until it was annexed to the City of Schenectady in 1902 as the Tenth Ward. A pleasant suburban settlement high on the southerly embankment overlooking the city, Bellevue was just beginning to undergo its greatest era of housing development as new streets were laid almost as fast as real estate agents parceled out building lots.

The reason, of course, was because of the booming business of the fledgling General Electric Company and the influx of families to meet the demand for more workers. It had been going on since Thomas A. Edison brought his electrical machine works to the Rotterdam flats in 1886, but was particularly acute after 1900 when the city population started an unprecedented upward swing. By 1910, there would be nearly 73,000 people living in Schenectady as compared to fewer than 20,000 in 1890.

Taking up residence in Bellevue had many advantages, including the fact that it was only a short distance down the old cinder path to the main General Electric plant. The growing community had a reputation for being "a nice place for families" with a new school (Euclid, built 1899), two churches, a main thoroughfare called Broadway, paved in 1909 only a few years after the electric cars began servicing the area, and a small park named Fairview. In those early days, Bellevue was dubbed the "Holy City" because its residents frowned on saloons in their midst and, for a time, succeeded in keeping them out.

As the Tenth Ward, Bellevue officially became urbanized nearly a century ago, but to this day Bellevuites feel closely attached to the Town of Rotterdam and its history. It's not easy, nor is it always desirable, to shed old ties.

With the influx of many families into the Bellevue neighborhoods, it was only natural that schools and churches soon followed. At the corner of Broadway and Genesee Street, the Bellevue Reformed Church was constructed upon its founding in 1893. This first church building is shown here in about 1900. At left is the brick Euclid School, built in 1899, and at right is the old District 2 School, built in 1888, enlarged in 1893 and burned in 1925.

Shortly after 1900, a new and striking Gothic-style Bellevue Reformed Church was erected and became the pride of Bellevue. It is shown here in 1956 shortly before reconstruction.

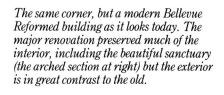

The same corner, but a modern Bellevue Reformed building as it looks today. The major renovation preserved much of the interior, including the beautiful sanctuary (the arched section at right) but the exterior is in great contrast to the old.

A hunter pauses in his trek through the Backus Woods in Bellevue before the turn of this century. The grounds, often used by small game hunters, was part of the large estate of the Rev. Dr. J. Trumbull Backus, early pastor of the First Presbyterian Church of Schenectady, who built a summer home on that summit probably about 1855. The house was still there, occupied by the three Backus daughters, Maria, Ellen, and Mary, when the Bellevue section began to be developed in the early 1900s.

The city's department of parks and recreation became interested in the Backus estate as a prospective public recreational spot and bought the property in 1923 from the Backus sisters. When opened in 1926, it was called Hillhurst Park after the name given that area by the Reverend Dr. Backus. Above, a group of young people enjoy a picnic in Hillhurst Park, almost on the spot where the house once stood.

Bellevue was widely unsettled when Julius Zander began his work as a blacksmith in a new shop built at the corner of Fairview Avenue and Broadway in the late 1880s. He is shown at right plying his trade outside his smithy about 1900.

Later, Zander's business was taken over by an assistant, Julius Zemke. (By strange coincidence, both men had the same surname, the same initials and were naturalized citizens of German heritage). This photo, made in 1924 by veteran photographer Will Underhill, shows the old shop just before it was demolished and replaced by a gasoline station. Zemke moved his business a block away, although there was less and less call for shoeing horses.

As the same corner looks today, still with a service station and food store. Fairview Avenue is at right, Broadway in the foreground. At right is a state historic marker that was installed in 1983 designating the spot as the site of Bellevue's first smithy.

The sidewalk ended at that corner and there were only a few houses on Fourth Street at left when this picture was made of John W. Hudson's hardware store soon after he had the Hudson Block constructed and opened for business in 1907. Broadway and the new trolley tracks are in the foreground. The Hudson family lived upstairs, where tenants leased other apartments.

The Hudson Hardware business was operated until 1964 for a total of fifty-seven years. John Hudson, who worked at the store part time after his retirement, died in 1961 at ninety-three. An electronic appliance store currently occupies the lower floor, as shown here, while the upper floors are still used for apartments. Needless to say, Fourth Street has long since been filled with homes.

*Shown here is the wood chapel built in December 1902 by the founding congregation of the Broadway Methodist Episcopal Church. The Reverend William Groat, second church pastor from 1908 to 1912, is standing in front.*

*Members of the first Ladies Aid Society of Broadway Methodist pose outside the chapel in 1905. Front row, from left, are Mrs. George Hodsoll, Mrs. M. T. Van Deusen, Mrs. W. N. Ingerson, Mrs. M. J. Osteyee (pastor's wife) and son, and Mrs. Barbara Crouse. Back row, from left, are Mrs. Charles Pink, the Reverend M. J. Osteyee, Mrs. August Schell, Mrs. W. J. Sisson, Mrs. R. A. Fisher, and Mrs. George Fisher.*

*The cornerstone laying ceremony for the new brick church of Broadway Methodist was held May 1, 1922—complete with band music and orators. As can be seen, a large crowd gathered for the occasion.*

*Now, sixty-six years later, the Broadway United Methodist Church remains one of Bellevue's impressive structures at the corner of Broadway and Bradt Street. The educational and office facility at right was added in recent years.*

*A New York Central train speeds toward the Carman grade crossing about 1920. The signal tower is at left, next the Hamburg Street. The old fire gong is beside it. Carman was known originally as Athens Junction when the Athens Railroad built a branch line in the 1850s to that junction with the New York Central.*

*John S. Barhydt, Sr. at the switch controls in the control tower farther east of the crossing. He was also the telegrapher. This picture dates to about 1910.*

# A Proud Township

The town of Rotterdam, named after the founding Dutch, is undergoing a revival in housing and business that is the envy of most parts of Schenectady County. Until its chartering as a town in 1820, the sprawling Rotterdam was a rural area known only as the city's Third Ward. It was sparsely settled, most of the inhabitants living in little settlements such as Athens Junction, South Schenectady, East Rotterdam, Rotterdam Junction, Mohawkville, and Pattersonville.

It has grown with the times, of course, but in the last two decades there has been a phenomenal increase in all facets of community progress—more industry, small businesses, housing developments, new streets, wider main routes, larger school districts and shopping centers.

Its inhabitants love parades and all kinds of celebrations. They will turn out for civic events en masse at the drop of a hat, and cheer the politicians they put in office. They especially support the slogan adopted by the town several years ago: "Rotterdam... A Nice Place to Live."

*Baryhydt (at right) crosses the tracks from the control tower after a day's work.*

*The same scene today from the Carman overhead bridge. Chrisler Avenue is in the background.*

*The Carman Methodist Church, completed in 1916, was on Hamburg Street nearly opposite Chepstow Street. It was much involved with civic affairs of the community and many early Carman residents were its members. By 1957, when this picture was made, the church was in need of expansion and an education building was erected on an opposite corner. Finally, the new Carman United Methodist Church building was constructed in 1967 adjoining the education building, leaving the old church vacant.*

*Finally, the original church building was demolished and now two new homes stand in its place, at 2319 and 2323 Hamburg Street.*

115

*Children playing in the front playground of Rotterdam School District 8, better known as John Bigsbee School, in 1925. The first schoolhouse on that site was built in 1825 for the sum of "57 dollars and fifty-six cents raised by taks."*

*John Bigsbee School had become much larger by 1953 when this picture was made. Now there was a large addition to the front, plus a gymnasium/cafeteria out of camera range to the left. Its days as an educational facility were numbered after July 1, 1955, when the area was centralized into the Mohonasen School District. However, it was used until 1979.*

*The Bigsbee property was purchased by Alfred DiBella, who remodeled the newer building (left) and opened a large restaurant known as DiBella's Restaurant and Home of Banquets. The schoolhouse in background was slated for demolition early in 1988, the space to be used to expand the restaurant's parking and outdoor catering facilities.*

Jefferson School pupils in the town of Rotterdam went almost directly across Princetown Road at Ford Avenue this chilly spring morning in 1951 to witness the cornerstone ceremony of their new school. When completed the following year, the school replaced the old District No. 11 School building, which was remodeled and converted into the Rotterdam Police Headquarters.

Jefferson School as it looks today, now thirty-seven years old but in excellent condition. The 1951 cornerstone can be seen in the lower right corner.

*Old District No. 14 School was one of Rotterdam's early schoolhouses, located on Guilderland Road extension just off Curry Road, near a malodorous slaughterhouse called the "hide house" by local citizens. The school burned in May, 1914, just as the Draper School was partially opened. In this picture, made about 1910, can be seen the outhouses in the yard at left.*

*The school site currently is occupied by this modern structure at 2806 Guilderland, which houses the Rotterdam Veterinary Hospital.*

The community of West Hill, off Putnam Road in the town of Rotterdam, was just being developed when this picture was made in 1953, looking up what was to be called Terrace Road. An army surplus generator in the right foreground furnished power for carpenters.

Above, Terrace Road as it looks today, in the midst of a picturesque neighborhood that even now bespeaks the comforts and beauty of modern architecture.

The Nine Mile Bridge along Route 5 as it looked in 1952, shortly before its demolition preparatory to reconstruction of that state highway. The bridge was so called because it was approximately nine miles from Schenectady and the same distance from Amsterdam. This view is westerly, so that it is just past the left entrance to the Lock No. 9 bridge to Rotterdam Junction. To the extreme left is the beginning of the roadway down to the Riverview Inn.

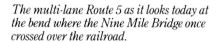

A 1938 picture of Hixon's Riverview Inn, located on the banks of the Mohawk River just beyond Lock No. 9. It enjoyed popularity through the 1930s and early 1940s as a restaurant with cabaret style entertainment until fire leveled it in the late 1940s.

The multi-lane Route 5 as it looks today at the bend where the Nine Mile Bridge once crossed over the railroad.

*The main street of Rotterdam Junction (later officially named Main Street), shown here about 1900, looked every bit the part of a farming community. Yet, there was much activity in all directions with the railroad junction in its midst to take over where the Erie Canal would end.*

*Another view westward along Rotterdam Junction's Main Street, this time about 1908.*

*A modern view along Main Street from Putnam Street, again looking westerly on Route 5-S in the direction of Pattersonville.*

The Mabee House, a popular hotel in
Rotterdam Junction through the years, is
shown in this westerly view along the
community's main street about 1880.

The same view today, with the historic
Mabee House, now an apartment building,
at left.

*Railroad men were steady boarders at the Vanderpool Hotel on Rotterdam Junction's Main Street, as shown here about 1890. It became known as the Railroad YMCA after the Fitchburg line was taken over by the Boston and Maine Railroad.*

*This was the building that replaced the old Vanderpool Hotel when it burned after the turn of the century. It, too, was known as the Railroad YMCA but in its later days— as shown here in 1947—it became the Victory Hotel.*

*Fire destroyed the Victory Hotel in the winter of 1949.*

*The old hotel site in Rotterdam Junction now is occupied by commercial buildings.*

*A view about 1890 of the Jones House in Lower Rotterdam Junction, once called East Rotterdam Junction. John Guenther, proprietor, is the man in the vest and white shirt standing at center. Mrs. Guenther is far left. Leaning on a post, right center, is William Peek. Courtesy of Allen J. Peek*

*The building is still there, along Route 5-S, but it has long since been known as Myers Tavern.*

## Glen Sanders Mansion

Reputed to be the oldest house in the Schenectady vicinity is the Glen Sanders Mansion in Scotia, originally built in 1658 by Alexander Lindsey Glen, a Scot who was the first white man to settle in the Mohawk Valley west of Fort Orange (Albany). His home was across the Mohawk River from where Schenectady would be founded in another three years. A major renovation, including a large front hall, was made in 1713 by Glen's heirs.

It is so much a part of Scotia's heritage that when the village was incorporated in 1904, the mansion was included in the official village seal.

*An old view of the Glen Sanders Mansion and grounds about 1880. It is unusual in that it shows the old barns and outbuildings on the property at that time. The low, swampy area in foreground had to be filled in when construction of the first Western Gateway Bridge began in 1922.*

*The house as it looked in 1900, along a front pathway leading from Glen Avenue.*

# The Village Across the River

Scotia, incorporated as a village in 1904, is directly across the Mohawk River from downtown Schenectady. Although a separate governmental entity, Scotia has always had close ties with Schenectady. As a matter of fact, it was the Fourth Ward of the city until it became part of Glenville when that township was formed in 1820.

Scotia was so named by its founder, Alexander Lindsey (of the Glen Estk in Scotland), an enterprising Scot who came to America in 1643 as an agent for the Dutch West India Company and decided to build on the west bank of the river in 1658 to be even closer to the fur trade in that Mohawk Indian territory. This was three years before Schenectady was settled on the east bank. When established April 14, 1820, the Glenville township was named in honor of the Glen family, Lindsey having early taken the name Glen as a surname.

As the actual gateway to the west, Scotia was part of the saga of the early growth and development of the Mohawk Valley. The Mohawk Turnpike went through it to Schenectady in 1804. Broom corn flourished along the Scotia flats in the early 1800s when the broom industry was a big business for the better part of that century. When the Schenectady Railway Company began to expand its city lines in 1902, the trolleys started going to Scotia over the old iron bridge. The first Western Gateway Bridge was an engineering achievement when it opened in late 1925, formally linking Scotia and Schenectady in the modern era. The second bridge would be opened forty-eight years later to the day: December 19, 1973.

Scotia residents are happy, content and proud of their village community. It has grown through the years, so much so that there are few vacant lots within its perimeter, but it still retains its "small town" image with private homes, clean streets, neighborliness, holiday celebrations and village hall meetings.

The dining room of the mansion is shown here about 1900 when electric lights were first installed. Many of these antiques were purchased by Colonial Williamsburg, Virginia, in 1965 after the last of the Sanders family sold the property. It became known as the Glen Sanders Mansion in 1739 when Debora Glen married John Sanders of Albany.

Today the house is in the same location on the eastern end of Scotia and next to the river, probably in better condition than it has ever been. It was on the verge of destruction through neglect when Dr. and Mrs. Dolph G. Ebeling purchased it and moved in in the early 1970s and made extensive restoration and repairs inside and out.

*Young Edward Martinec, on his way to school guard duty in 1929, poses with his dog, Lump, on Mohawk Avenue in Scotia. A horse watering trough is at right curbside. The old village post office is across the street, above Edward's head.*

*Edward Martinec borrowed a neighbor's dog, Bow, to simulate the pose of fifty-eight years previous. A decorated infantry soldier of World War II, he recently retired from the grocery business begun by his father more than seventy years ago.*

People in the "olden days" liked to pose in front of their homes, usually with the horse-drawn rig, and Daniel Henry Slover was no exception. Here, in this picture of about 1910, he's seated in his buggy outside his house at 212 Mohawk Avenue in Scotia. All six of his living (and married) children are lined up on the tiny porch—Rosella, Elma, Cora, Caroline, Roy and Edith.

The tiny house is still in good shape at the same address. The front downstairs section has been converted into a barbershop run by Dominick B. DaMassa.

Daniel C. Minor was manager of the Scotia
Motor Sales & Garage at 110 Mohawk
Avenue when this picture was made about
1922. It was typical of service availability to
motorists of that day. A curbside gasoline
pump, handcranked with the familiar glass
dome, was a sign that help was near if
garage work was needed.

Today, the same building has been
expanded to the left and rear and for many
years has been the home of Scotia Motors,
Inc. The house at left was included in the
expansion and the peak of the roof is partly
visible at top center.

131

Scotia's first post office was located in a tiny
structure at 109 Mohawk Avenue, a few
doors above Ballston Avenue.

One of the village's earliest letter carriers of
the 1890s, unidentified to date.

*The house of James M. Willis at 224 Mohawk Avenue, near the corner of Center Street at right, is shown here in the 1920s. It was demolished in 1939 to make way for the new Scotia Post Office.*

*Opened in 1940, the Scotia Post Office as it looks today.*

*Believed to have been a carriage house for the Mohawk Turnpike in the early 1800s, this old wood building at the corner of Mohawk Avenue and North Ballston Avenue was known in later years as the Rose Block after Dr. Wilber S. Rose bought it. For many years, the lower floor was a grocery store run by Lansing and Livingstone Slover. This view is about 1915.*

*The same building as it looked in the 1930s when it was slated for demolition.*

*Montana's service station has occupied that same corner since shortly after the old Rose Block was removed.*

134

For many years, up until it finally was modified in 1949, a railroad bridge on North Ballston Avenue in Scotia was a hazard to travelers using that Route 50 byway. This 1936 view looks northerly from Scotia up to the bridge, which crosses the former New York Central Railroad tracks. The Boston & Maine tracks cross overhead. In the foreground are the tracks of the Fonda, Johnstown & Gloversville interurban trolleys, which occasionally were involved in accidents at that point.

From the downslope of the old bridge, again in 1936, looking toward the village. The trolleys had stopped running by this time, but the narrow road and blind corner from Cuthbert Street at right still caused problems.

Not only was a new bridge constructed, beginning in 1949, but the approaches were altered so that a more direct route was made between the village and Thomas Corners intersection of Route 50. The road also was widened. Above, workers construct a new bridge crossing for the Boston & Maine tracks over Route 50.

As it looks today. The road from the foreground to right leads to where the old bridge had been. The new bridge, under the Boston & Maine crossing, is at far left.

*A startling contrast is presented here in two views about a century apart on what is now the west corner of Vley Road and Halcyon Street in Scotia. The photo above is of the old Veeder "Fort" in 1890, said to be an outpost of the old Schenectady fort and in use until after the American Revolution. It was occupied by Nicholas Veeder, a revolutionary war soldier, and later by his son Abraham. The picture below shows the corner as it looks today.*

*Once a familiar sight to people who stopped by the bridge at Sunnyside Road to watch passing trains, the big brick roundhouse of the New York Central Railroad was part of a busy environment in that area after the turn of the century.*

*This is the so-called Sandbank area off Sunnyside Road in Scotia, now a deserted site. The roundhouse was demolished in 1952.*

This picture was made by a White Studio photographer on February 12, 1927, at Thomas Corners in East Glenville—only three days after the Schenectady Chamber of Commerce announced that land had been optioned there for development of the Schenectady Airport. Route 50 is in the foreground and the junction of Freeman's Bridge Road is just beyond it at center. The airport land is in the far background.

This is the Thomas Corners junction as it looks today. The airport is still in the background, but many other commercial ventures have grown up around it as well.

The Schenectady County Airport was known as Port Schenectady when it first opened in 1927, although unfinished. One of its first visitors was Col. Charles A. Lindbergh and his "Spirit of St. Louis" on July 28, 1927, during his goodwill tour of American cities. The above view of the main hangar is of June, 1928. Courtesy of White Studio

Crowds often gathered at the airport on weekends to watch the "aeroplanes" come and go. This was also the summer of 1928.

The old control/observation tower at the Schenectady County Airport as it burned during an early morning rainstorm on April 7, 1953.

142

*This aerial view of the airport shows the public section at lower right, along Route 50, while the base of the 109th Tactical Airlift Group, Air National Guard, is at top left.*

*An estimated 55,000 spectators turned out for the closing day of the Northeast Flight '87 Airshow held at Schenectady County Airport on August 29 and 30, 1987. Part of the crowd is shown above with the National Guard's C-141 "Starlifter" mammoth transport plane. Courtesy of the* Schenectady Gazette

*Endries Inn on Saratoga Road in East Glenville was a highly popular place for banquets, wedding receptions and outdoor cookouts and clambakes for much of the 1920s and 1930s. It even had an 18-hole golf course at the back of the establishment. Green fees were fifty cents a round. Actually, Endrie's began in 1924 when Joseph and Elizabeth Endries bought some farm property on Route 50 and converted a barn into the inn. Endries Inn prospered until overrun by the building boom in the early 1960s.*

*The inn and its expansive grounds were sold by the last owners, Edward and Ann Zelmer, in 1963 to developers of Willowbrook Homes. It was demolished that same year and work began immediately on construction of Willowbrook Shopping Plaza. In this picture, the Willowbrook sign at center stands approximately on the site of the former inn. Route 50 is in the foreground of both photos.*

The High Mills section of Burnt Hills along Route 50 got its name from the lumber mill, which in the nineteenth century operated alongside the Alplaus Creek, dammed up at the mill site to provide power. Several wood bridges had been constructed in earlier years to allow passage of horse-driven vehicles, but a wood and steel span, shown here about 1915, was constructed in the 1890s for heavier traffic. This view is looking downstream from the mill.

Here is an upstream look at the mill at left and the dam in the background, with the old bridge overhead. This was such a picturesque area, with cataracts and miniature waterfalls, that the Schenectady Railway Company's 1905 travel brochure recommended stopping off at High Mills during an interurban trip.

Today, the bridge built in the 1930s handles a sizeable volume of traffic along Route 50, which is between Schenectady and Saratoga Springs. In this picture, the Alplaus Creek flows quite peaceably but in the spring it is a raging torrent. The old bridge and dam were a short distance upstream from here.

A northerly view looking across the bridge from Paradowski Road. Kristel Inn, a popular eating establishment since the 1920s, is located across the ravine at right, alongside the creek.

146

Shortly after the turn of this century, the residents of Burnt Hills—a Saratoga County community just north of Glenville—used the hardware/general store of Stevens & Sharpley as an information center. Not only was it the location of their post office, a small section of the store at left, but a favorite gathering place as well. The building burned on Memorial Day, 1924, but the business was last operated by Nate Seeley and Isaac Sharpley.

The same corner site at Lakehill and Kingsley roads as it looks today, now the location of what is known as "Village Corner," or Geyer Office Complex.

*Freeman's Bridge Road in East Glenville was a quiet country road when this picture was made about 1900. The home beneath the trees in center background was once the summer home of Charles Ellis, president of the Schenectady Locomotive Works, and later was taken over by his daughter and son-in-law, Mr. and Mrs. James W. Yelverton. Maple Avenue, the road to Alplaus, is at right center.*

*A farewell party for Schenectady men of the 105 Infantry Machine Gun Company was given by the Yelvertons at their country place in the summer of 1917, shortly before the group left for combat in Europe.*

148

*The house was purchased in 1922 by milk dealer K. C. Sarnowski who opened a dairy business there known as Sarnowski Farms. The dwelling and its picturesque barns graced that corner for many years until, years after Sarnowski's death, the property slowly fell into disrepair. The barns burned down several years ago. This view of April 1987, was one month before the house was demolished.*

*A Stewart's bread and butter store was erected on the site within a matter of weeks. This is the corner as it looks today.*

The Niskayuna Reformed Church was founded in 1790 when the Reverend John Demerest came to preach to residents of that area. A small church building was erected but the large brick edifice still in use at 3041 Troy Road was dedicated March 8, 1829. The old parsonage (still in use) alongside the church is shown here in 1885. Shown are Reverend Cornelius Ditmar, his wife, their son Charles and daughter Ida, with Emma Schairer.

*The parsonage today.*

# Three Oldest Townships

When Schenectady County was founded in 1809, mostly from lands originally part of Albany County of colonial days, three townships were chartered that same year. They were Niskayuna, named from Indian terminology meaning "fields of corn"; Duanesburg, named after its principal early citizen, Judge James Duane; and Princetown, named after John Prince of Schenectady, a member of the state assembly.

Each has its own beauty and attributes as suburban, even rural settlements. The picturesque rolling hills of Princetown and Duanesburg are a sight to behold at any time of the year, but most particularly in the fall when tinted foliage brightens the countryside. These two have remained mostly rural, some of the inhabitants proudly claiming that their forebears farmed the same hills two centuries ago.

Niskayuna, adjoining the city of Schenectady to the northeast, has the distinction of being a three-in-one township. It is rural, suburban, and urban, depending on which part of the town one happens to reside. Its large high school supports all kinds of sports and is proud of academic achievement. In the area east of Ellis Hospital, it is difficult to tell where the city leaves off and the town begins. In other sections, on upper Union Street and along Balltown Road for example, the development is purely high-class suburban. Farther out Troy Road, River Road or Consaul Road and it's rural living.

Niskayuna, Duanesburg and Princetown, in their own right, give Schenectady County a flair for complete living it would not otherwise have.

*The church congregation at the annual church picnic in the early 1900s. This outing was held in the woods once located at the corner of Mill Road and Troy Road.*

*The Niskayuna Reformed Church building today...much as it looked nearly 150 years ago.*

152

A single-truck trolley car waits beside the passenger hut of the Rosa Road stop in 1905, ready to begin the return trip downtown to the General Electric works. In the background was the first course of the Mohawk Golf Club, bounded roughly by present-day Lenox Road, Raymond Street, Rosa Road and Nott Street, and which then lay idle. The club moved up to its present location off Troy Road the year before and now the former golf course would be developed into elegant homes and streets.

Rosa Road as it looks today at that spot, the whole section where the golf course existed now considered part of the prestigious GE Realty Plot development, now a historic district. At right is one of the entrances to Ellis Hospital, which moved there in 1906.

In 1906, Ellis Hospital had moved from Jay Street in downtown Schenectady up to a new location on what was called Corlaer Heights. Shown here upon its completion, an unpaved Nott Street is in the foreground. The building at left of the hospital is the Whitmore Home for Nurses off Rosa Road, constructed at the same time as the hospital. This was Schenectady's first hospital, established on Christmas Day, 1885, as a public dispensary at 408 Union Street.

Now, more than a century since its founding, Ellis Hospital has expanded numerous times on the Corlaer Heights location as additions were made through the years as patient usage demanded it. Even a multi-tier parking garage (right) was erected by 1978 to alleviate the visitor parking problem. More construction is anticipated. Part of the original section of 1906 is in the center foreground. Courtesy of Ellis Hospital

The glass negative from which this print was made was labeled "Rexford apple pickers, 1911" with no identification of the four young ladies.

However, we do have the names of the three modern apple pickers shown here with part of the 1987 fall harvest at Barrett's Riverview Orchards in Rexford. They are the daughters of J. Howard Barrett, who started the business in 1945. From left are Isabel Prescott, Phyllis Holzhauer and Evelyn Prouty.

*Time had nearly run out on this schoolhouse in 1952 as children enjoyed the playground slide. Rexford School was closed soon after consolidation of the Niskayuna School District the next year. Even though the community of Rexford is just inside Saratoga County, it falls within the Niskayuna School District.*

*The Rexford schoolhouse was used for a time as a storage area for school supplies, but in a few years its place at the corner of Route 146 and Riverview Road was taken by the Rexford Fire District Station.*

*Captioned only "On a Duanesburg Meadow," this old print of early picnickers, probably about 1910, is typical of the earlier times when folks just stopped their carriage or automobile and spread a blanket on the ground for a repast.*

# This and That

There are highlights and sidelights to every story. Although the story of changes within a city and its environs naturally stress the metamorphism of streets, buildings and material things, there are also degrees of change in such things as public works, transportation, even social graces, that have a bearing on the subject.

How interesting it is to look back on what we now consider archaic by our present standards, but we should not scoff. In years to come, others will be seeing us in the same light.

Today, we have parks and rest stops where travelers can enjoy picnics with the convenience of tables, fireplaces and mowed grass. Above, a group of young people enjoy an afternoon at John Boyd Thacher Park, a New York State Park, in Albany County.

Dr. Eleanor Mann, general practitioner in the Schenectady area for many years earlier this century, always preferred a horse and carriage (or sleigh) to make house calls. Here, she is shown in 1918 in front of her home and office at 2 Lowell Road.

On the other hand, Dr. Elizabeth Van Rensselaer Gillette forsook her horse-drawn conveyance for this two-cylinder 1906 Maxwell. Her home and office were located at 234 Union Street. Dr. Gillette, also a GP, practiced in Schenectady until retirement in 1959.

Modern medicine and transportation befits Dr. Robin Rahm, surgeon, shown in the parking lot of Community Health Plan's Latham headquarters on Troy Road, Niskayuna.

*This is the same building as it looks today.*

*Dr. E. F. Alexanderson at his Adams Road home in 1928 with his early television apparatus. That same year, he gave a public demonstration in Proctor's Theatre of the wonders of television.*

## Old Time Bakeries

For certain, one thing that must be uppermost in childhood memories is the neighborhood bakery, where the most delicious smell of fresh-baked goods lingered with haunting fragrance. We can remember our first encounter there with a jelly doughnut, lady finger, gingerbread man, or a chocolate eclair.

Schenectady has had its share of such enticing establishments as far back as the pre-revolutionary days. Many of the early shops delivered baked goods either by handcart, bicycle wagon, or a horse-drawn wagon. It was the latter that many people remember today—even before most of the home deliveries dwindled down to Freihofer, Kannaley and Waldorf.

Finally, it was left to the Charles Freihofer Baking Company, which continued home deliveries by the familiar red wagon pulled by a horse savvy to the route. In 1958, however, the house-to-house routes were abandoned and thereafter people bought their bread and cake at markets or area bake shops. Some of the better known ones downtown of the thirties and forties were those of Electrik Maid, Federal Bake Shops, Italian United, Perreca's, Joseph Pitts, Edward Dawson, White Eagle, and United Baking Company.

From the number of old-time pictures showing a bakery owner posed proudly beside his delivery wagon, one can only surmise either that there was an enterprising photographer lurking about or simply that it was "the thing to do."

*Richard Long, a Schenectady youngster, poses beside his friend, a Freihofer Baking Company horse, about 1915.*

*Driver George Kilmer eases his horse-drawn bakery wagon into the Albany Street plant at the end of a day in July 1948.*

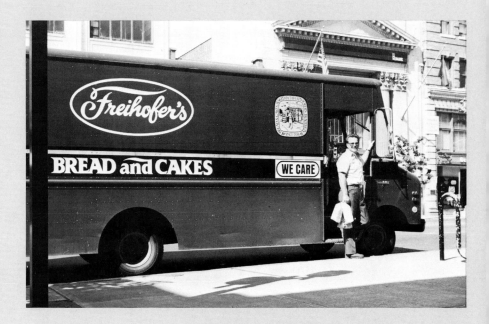

*Howard Mangum, driver of a Freihofer delivery truck, making his rounds of State Street restaurants and shops in downtown Schenectady. Home deliveries stopped 30 years ago when the horse-drawn wagons were taken off the routes.*

*The Charles Freihofer Baking Company came to Schenectady in 1915 when it built its new plant at 1238 Albany Street. Above is a view of the construction site.*

*The Schenectady plant today, now a storage and thrift shop center because the baking is done in Albany. The company, which first opened in Troy in 1913, was sold to the General Foods Corporation in August 1987 for well over $100 million. However, it is expected that the Freihofer name for the baker will continue despite the sale.*

*Alfred Stoodley is shown at right beside his delivery wagon and outside his bakery at Union Street and Fonda Street shortly after he began business there in 1890. His was a popular bakery up until his retirement in 1936.*

*That same corner today, except that Fonda Street at right has long since been renamed North Jay Street. Jo-Jo's Auto Service now occupies the Stoodley Bakery site.*

*A. L. Chadsey outside his bake shop at 721
State Street. It was a mark of distinction to
strike such a pose. This was about 1900.*

*The present site of 721 State Street,
formerly Chadsey's bakery, on the rise just
above Nott Terrace.*

170

*Another proud bakery owner, W. N. Butler, in his delivery wagon on Hamilton Street. He was among Schenectady's bakers of nearly a century ago. His shop was at 713 Albany Street, nearly opposite Summit Avenue where he lived.*

171

The Centre Street Opera House, which opened March 19, 1888, a few days after the great blizzard, never reached the potential as a local live theater attraction that its backers had hoped. It booked a variety of shows, ranging from operettas and drama to boxing matches and magicians. This view is of its early days, complete with cobblestone paving and bricked sidewalks.

# Theaters of Old

The old movie houses were like old friends but, sadly, for those who can remember them, most are gone.

They began as the "flickers" by the turn of this century, often in social halls or lodge meeting rooms, wherever movable chairs could be set up to face a cloth screen placed on a wall. Then came the bona fide theaters, first in the downtown section but shortly after emerging in residential areas as neighborhood theaters.

Schenectady had a goodly share of movie theaters in the halcyon years of motion pictures. In 1939, there were still five large ones downtown and nine of the "locals" scattered throughout the other city wards. Some of the earlier ones had already been closed. But, as social habits and even movies themselves began to change in the 1950s, the old established theaters began playing to nearly empty houses.

One by one, they folded. Some were taken over by other businesses, others were converted into parking lots. Meanwhile, the movie trade went to compact theaters built near the suburban shopping malls where the younger set congregated and were more likely to support the new trend in motion pictures.

The fate of some of the favorite movie theaters in Schenectady are related in the following. Not all, of course. It would be too boring for some and depressing for others.

Opened in 1912 as the first Proctor's
Theatre in downtown Schenectady, the big
vaudeville house located alongside the Erie
Canal went through numerous stages in its
lifetime. It was mostly live theater at the
outset, although motion pictures were
coming on strong. After the new Proctor's
was constructed by 1926 farther up State
Street, the old one was renamed the
Wedgeway after the adjoining building. Still
later, it was named the Erie. Above is an
early photo of the foyer with typical
embellishments of that period.

The curtain was really coming down in this
picture made at the time of the Erie Theater
demolition in 1957. The dozer operator at
left is clearing rubble from battered walls.

*From the Erie Boulevard side during demolition, the huge wall of the auditorium (there were two balconies) at left and the stage loft at right are shown.*

*Cars are parked now at the corner where the old Erie once stood.*

A row of mid-eighteenth century brick
homes on the south side of Liberty Street
between Ferry Street and Erie Boulevard
were leveled in the spring of 1953 to provide
additional parking at the rear of State Street
businesses. Here they are shown as
salvageable material was removed before
demolition.

The State Theater, built in 1922, was
hardly used and partially maintained after
its closing in the mid-1960s. An arcade
from State Street to Liberty Street had
featured small shops as well as entrance to
either the Erie or State theaters. The
deteriorating auditorium of the once-ornate
State Theater is shown in April 1984.
*Courtesy of* Schenectady Gazette

*The roof of the State Theater was being dismantled in this picture of May 5, 1985. Courtesy of* Schenectady Gazette

*Now, with the exception of the newly remodeled Barney Square in the center background, the south side of Liberty Street in that section is completely given over to parking.*

The Strand Theater on Barrett Street, just
a few doors in from State, began in 1921 as
the Barcli—a name using the combination
of the two streets it abutted, Barrett and
Clinton. In 1930, it was renamed the
Strand. For some reason, the Strand never
seemed to enjoy the popularity of other large
downtown movie houses but it was in
business until a final closing in 1953.
Above is a 1956 picture showing the front
entrance on Barrett Street with State Street
at far left. Upstairs, three floors above the
theater foyer was Cain's Castle, a dance hall
run by dance instructor Francis Cain.

The scene today. The theater building was
demolished in 1972 when construction
began on the Schenectady branch of the
Albany Savings Bank on State Street
between Clinton and Barrett. Also razed for
the new construction were the former
Niagara Mohawk Power Corporation office
building and the five-story Lorraine Block.

The RKO Plaza Theater was opened
August 28, 1931, with a good turnout to see
Maurice Chevalier in "The Smiling
Lieutenant." Located on the State Street
hill across from former Crescent Park (now
Veterans Park), the theater quickly grew to
be one of the favorites among the downtown
movie houses. Its striking interior, a
Grecian garden motif with blinking stars
and scudding clouds on the blue ceiling
overhead, gave patrons an exotic treat.

*These were the ushers of the Plaza at the time it opened, all dressed in their uniforms and posed on the sidewalk outside the theater.*

*A matinee crowd outside the Plaza in this picture of the 1950s belies the fact that the Plaza, along with other movie theaters of that time, was in big trouble. There just wasn't enough patronage to warrant staying open. Social habits in the entertainment field were changing, among them staying home to watch television, and the movies were suffering the consequences. The Plaza did stay open until after the Labor Day performance in 1963 and was torn down a year later.*

*Arrangements had been made before the Plaza's demolition for a motor lodge firm to build on the site, but the deal fell through and the lot (center) is still empty. The First United Methodist Church at Lafayette Street is at left.*

When the new Proctor's Theatre opened December 27, 1926, patrons were agog over its magnificent trappings, enormous auditorium, and the mighty Wurlitzer pipe organ, which filled the place with soul-stirring sound. Above is an exterior view of the front marquee in 1927, bathed in General Electric floodlighting.

This was the interior of the theater hall in 1927, quite in keeping with the huge movie palaces being built in that era.

The front entrance of Proctor's Theatre
today... completely restored, inside and out.

Proctor's underwent some bad times in the
fifties and sixties, changing management
several times and finally being closed for tax
delinquency. Luckily, the Arts Center and
Theatre of Schenectady (ACTS) was formed
in 1977 and two years later purchased the
theater for one dollar from the City of
Schenectady. From then to now, the theater
has attained a reputation as a one-of-a-kind
theatrical experience in this part of the
country, featuring vaudeville, top stage
productions, organ recitals, band, orchestra
and chorale concerts, and sound and silent
movies. Above, a volunteer worker is shown
hard at work in the top mezzanine restoring
some of Proctor's former elegance.

The Rivoli Theater at 1615 Union Street was an attractive, yet typical neighborhood movie theater that brought delight and entertainment to the families of upper Union Street after the mid-1920s. It had the usual Saturday matinees for children, double features and such patron inducements as free dishes, groceries and talent shows during the Great Depression. However, it was entering its dwindling days in this photo of the early 1950s as were old-style movie houses everywhere.

The former theater has long since been converted to other commercial uses. Currently, it houses a physical fitness center, a pet shop and a clothing store. Memories of the Rivoli still remain as grandparents tell young audiences of the days when they saw some memorable black-and-white films right there in that same building.

182

The Odd Fellows Hall at Broadway and Thompson Street in Bellevue, shown here in a postcard view of about 1910, has become a landmark of that area. Older residents recall the days in the "flickers" era when they watched the early silent movies in the downstairs hall of the Bellevue IOOF Headquarters. When used for that purpose, it was called the Cozy Theater.

The old hall has undergone many changes over the years, but it remains a part of Bellevue's activities. It has been taken over by the Immaculate Conception Church, which is located on Thompson Street, and is used currently as a Bingo hall and for church social functions. A new siding and realignment of the front entrance has altered the building's appearance.

The Cameo Theater was a typical favorite neighborhood theater for families of the Bellevue area from the time it was built in 1922 until the waning days of movie houses in the 1950s. Located at 2226 Broadway, it was a vast improvement over the earlier movie houses in Bellevue, namely the Broadway near the top of the Broadway hill and the Cozy Theater in the Odd Fellows Hall at Thompson Street in those early days of the silent pictures and pianist. Saturday afternoon matinees, with spellbinding serials and oaters, were a must for the small fry.

A parking lot today marks the site of the once popular Cameo Theater, which was demolished by 1960.

184

The Lincoln Theater on South Brandywine Avenue was among the favorite neighborhood movie theaters since it was constructed in 1917. Its popularity lasted through most of the 1940s but had to close after the 1953 season because of dwindling attendance. Shown here is a matinee line in the late 1940s. The Albany Street corner is at left.

Detroit Electric first purchased the theater and converted the premises into a store and shop area. Now, the theater building (center) has been attached to a showroom addition for Cocca's, an appliances firm.

*The Broadway Theater, at 1740 Broadway, which showed the early silents, has long been a welding school and body works.*

*The Brandywine Theater, at 1301 Albany Street, also was a silent film theater that long ago became an auto body shop.*

The Central Park Theater, at 827 McClellan Street, saw both silent and sound film service but has been a commercial building for over half a century.

The Star Theater, at 1481 State Street, faded by the thirties and has since been used for a variety of businesses—currently an Oriental restaurant.

*The Colony Theater, at 1330 State Street, was a big neighborhood favorite for nearly sixty years. It last showed X-rated movies but has been vacant for almost a decade.*

*The Pearl Theater, at 735 Crane Street atop the hill, was an early silent movie house that has held many businesses since it closed in 1931. The current occupant is Marcella's Appliances.*

*The Scotia Cinema, at 117 Mohawk Avenue, Scotia, started in 1929 as the Ritz Theater...and is still around.*

*The American Theater at 776 Albany Street was a popular neighborhood movie house for half a century but in the 1960s, it became the headquarters for American Electric Supply Company.*

*The Erie Canal presents a peaceful scene in downtown Schenectady, about 1900, looking north toward the State Street bridge. The tow path is as left, Dock Street at right.*

*Now, a century later, the canal route has been Erie Boulevard for over sixty years and one of the city's busiest thoroughfares ever since.*

# The Erie Canal

As early as 1810, surveyors were in Schenectady beginning to map out the route of what was to be called the Erie Canal but what most citizens at first laughingly referred to as Clinton's Ditch. (Governor DeWitt Clinton was its principal backer.) Actually, there were few people around in those days who thought the project would materialize or, after it did, gave it much chance of success. Even President Thomas Jefferson, when hearing of the venture for the first time, said it was "sheer madness."

Although the official opening of the waterway was celebrated in 1825, Schenectady's section was linked from Albany to Little Falls and in operation by 1822. As a result, life changed considerably for a populace accustomed to reliance upon horse, oxen and river boats for transportation and freight hauling. The railroading age was not far off, yet the Erie Canal would have a sizeable impact on Schenectady's industrial and social life for nearly a century. Communities such as Rexford, Woestina and Pattersonville also grew and prospered along with the canal's operation.

The old Erie sliced through a portion of Schenectady's downtown, influencing commerce and industry in that area for many years. Somewhere about 1890, probably most city officials and its residents would just as soon be rid of the canal. It had outlived its usefulness as a freightway, long since as a passenger route, and now was relegated to a part-time conveyor of straggling barges and a place for folks to swim in during the summer and skate upon in the winter.

Finally, the end came in 1915 when the Erie Barge Canal system opened, making use of natural waters such as the Mohawk River and various midstate lakes with the embellishment of modern locks along the route—again, from the Hudson River to Lake Erie. But it was not until 1925, a hundred years after the Erie Canal opening, that the erstwhile canal bed became what was proclaimed the "biggest, widest, best-lit boulevard in the country."

Appropriately, it was named Erie Boulevard.

The Erie Canal tow path, in this photograph of about 1880, leads northward through Schenectady toward the Jefferson Street bridge in the center background. George Maxon's ten-story grain elevator is to the right just beyond the bridge, while the Delaware & Hudson Railroad freight office and warehouse is at right.

A look farther northward from Jefferson Street is provided by this unusual view on a glass negative, supposedly by early photographer Henry Tripp in 1880. It is surmised that he set up his equipment in the cupola of the Maxon grain elevator. The canal is in center, the Mohawk River to the left. Few houses were located west of the canal then, but by 1901 the American Locomotive Company would expand its works to that side.

A busy Erie Boulevard has marked the route of the canal through the city since the roadway was opened with great ceremony in the spring of 1925. The Jefferson Street corner is at right.

*An overview of the Erie Canal and Rexford locks in the foreground leading to the aqueduct in the left background, which crossed the Mohawk River. The village of Rexford is in the far background. This photograph is from about 1890.*

*The approximate same vantage point as it looks today. The boat yard of the Schenectady Yacht Club now occupies the canal and locking area, the aqueduct is long gone, and a new bridge crosses the Mohawk River at left as part of Route 146.*

*Erie Canal lock tenders and bargemen pose in front of Mickey Travis' saloon and restaurant in this view of 1908 at Lock No. 22 at Rexford.*

*The former saloon somehow survived the vast changes that took place after the original canal ceased operations after 1915. Today it is the headquarters of the Schenectady Yacht Club and one of the many historic buildings in Rexford.*

The village of Rexford forms a backdrop for this photograph of about 1900, looking north over the aqueduct of the Erie Canal as it crossed the Mohawk River toward Lock No. 22 in right background. McLane's Hotel, the building with a cupola just right of center, had become a landmark long before it was razed in 1964 when reconstruction of Route 146 began. The vehicle and pedestrian bridge to the left of the aqueduct was wrecked in the flood of March 1914.

Route 146 looking northward toward Rexford is a far different scene now from when the canal plied its route across the river. The original aqueduct bridge was to the right of the span shown at center, which was constructed in 1965 when Route 146 was altered and widened.

*The Edison Machine Works in 1889 as viewed easterly across old River Road and the Erie Canal. Then in its third year of operation, the plant was just beginning to grow.*

*A modern view from the approximate same location, now the multi-lane Thruway Spur.*

# Tom Edison's Legacy

The Age of Electricity actually made its first impact on Schenectady in the summer of 1885 when electric carbon arc street lamps were installed along downtown State Street from Church to Jay streets. However, it was to be the following year that a canal town would experience an event that would propel it to industrial heights within the decade.

Famed inventor Thomas Alva Edison decided in mid-1886 to move his electrical machine works out of New York City and up to Schenectady, settling in two unused brick factory buildings with plans to expand as production dictated. Here he had a ready labor market, no threat of unionizing, no demanding landlord, room for expansion, and a canal and railroad at his doorstep. It was a move that also proved greatly beneficial to Schenectady. Combined with the Schenectady Locomotive Works, it would not be long before Schenectady would become known as "the city that lights and hauls the world."

The electrical works grew rapidly, both in factories and employment. It became the Edison General Electric Company in 1890 and the General Electric Company in 1892, with the main plant at Schenectady. As the works prospered and grew, so did Schenectady. Both shared honors that came from General Electric's pioneering achievements in radio,

television, lighting, turbines, industrial research, and those many products that amazed the public so many years ago—things like the electric toaster, refrigerator, electric stove, electric hair curler, heaters, etc.

It has been just over a century since Edison set up shop in Schenectady. The 1980s probably have seen the biggest slowdown in orders and production in General Electric's history, the Great Depression included. Drastic steps have been taken to combat this downturn. Departments have been centralized, some buildings demolished, and cost-saving policies enforced. Employees have been encouraged to take early retirement while the work force has been gradually lessened. It was anticipated that 2,400 would be laid off in 1987, lowering the work force at the Schenectady plant to 12,400. During its peak years, that number was about 22,000.

Few citizens who have come and gone in these past one hundred years could deny that General Electric has been its greatest community asset. Nonetheless, more community leaders are beginning to stress the need for greater diversity of local businesses and employment rather than be overly dependent upon a major industry. The new century could be as exciting in Schenectady as the last.

*There was plenty of room for walkways and flower beds at the entrance to the works in the early 1890s when the General Electric Company was still in the formative stage. The guard house was then at Edison Avenue in the left background where visitors were checked for passes.*

First shift workers are shown leaving the main plant in Schenectady in this picture made from Building No. 5 in 1917. Edison Avenue is in the background. The old Westinghouse Agricultural Machinery Works buildings are at left.

The same avenue seventy years later. Building No. 2 is still at right, but IGE Building No. 36 at left has long since replaced the farm machinery factory. In the far background is the overhead roadway of Interstate 890.

*A view of General Electric's Works Avenue from Building No. 2 (at left) in 1904. Two small electric automobiles are parked in front of the office building.*

*Workers entering the main gate in 1946. Building No. 2 is at left.*

*The lower part of the main plant of General Electric about 1910 as viewed from the hill overlooking Broadway and Kruesi Avenue.*

*In the early 1920s, Thomas Edison met with several General Electric officials at his laboratory office in Orange, New Jersey. From left are J. W. Lieb, E. W. Rice Jr., Edison, George F. Morrison, and Gerard Swope.*

Standing before what was once the formal entrance to the campus atop the hill, these dandies of the mid-1870s pose with justifiable dignity at either side of the Blue Gate nearly atop Union Street hill. The entrance leads through the center background past the college president's house and along the terrace past South College and North College dorms to Nott Street beyond.

*The Blue Gate is a well-respected and revered fixture at Union College, but for many years has been open to vehicular traffic only for special occasions.*

# Union College

Before it was chartered in 1795, Union College's founding board seriously considered naming it Clinton College after George Clinton, New York's first governor.

It may well be that the influence of the First (Dutch) Reformed Church of Schenectady, which had in reality relinquished its own sponsored Schenectady Academy in favor of a higher institution, prevailed in the end. The dogmatic separation of church and state could have dictated the selection of a name not so obviously political.' Regardless, Union College received its charter and began classes in the former academy building at the northwest corner of Union and Ferry streets, moving into a new college facility a block east within the decade, and by 1814 relocating for good in the large "uptown" campus, which today is fairly close to the center of Schenectady's boundaries.

Through the years, the local citizenry has become increasingly proud of the fact that Union College is within its midst. It was an especially auspicious occasion when, in 1972 (two years after the college broke with tradition and went co-

educational), Union's campus was selected for the late-1930s segments of the movie, "The Way We Were." The real tie, however, is the community's participation in annual events—such as the Alumni Day parade, Homecoming weekend, Christmas festival, and commencement. They became a part of city life long before public education was established in Schenectady in 1854.

Union's campus remained fairly unchanged for many years, perhaps with the exception of the construction of Alumni Gymnasium in 1914 and Memorial Chapel in 1925. After the mid-1960s, an extensive rebuilding program began that involved demolition of some storied fixtures (Washburn Hall in particular) and construction of modern facilities, such as the Schaffer Library and Plaza, Social Sciences Building, Achilles Rink, a new Alexander Field, Alumni Fieldhouse and several dormitories. The domed 16-sided Nott Memorial, completed in 1875 and now entered in the National Register of Historic Places, still looks down upon these newcomers with a certain aplomb reserved for the old guard.

The sixteen-sided Nott memorial on Union's campus has become something of a symbol of its dignity and solidarity as one of America's leading small colleges. Although in the process of building before the Civil War, actual construction did not commence until 1872 as shown above and was fully completed two years later.

The domed structure has been used for many things through the years—a museum, classroom, storage facility, library, and now a Mountebanks theater with a book store and gift shop on the ground floor. It has been named to the National Register of Historic Places, although campus officials are concerned about a reported need for major reconstruction. Courtesy of Ed Schultz

206

Here is an unusual 1890 view of the Union College campus looking east from the roof of a grain elevator. A football game is in progress (center) on the library field. In full view are the few campus buildings of that day, from left: North College dorm, the chemistry lab, Washburn Hall, Nott Memorial, the old gym, Hale House, South College dorm and the president's house.

A recent aerial view of Union's campus, showing most but not all new construction.

# Postscript

For someone who has been researching and writing Schenectady's history for well over thirty years, the production of this book has proved an eye-opening experience.

Not until one has the opportunity to gather material for a then-and-now theme, covering not just a part, but the whole scene, can one realize how time in truth changes all things...right before one's eyes. That is exactly what happened to me since a little over a year ago, when I agreed to do this book.

Roughly, the plan was to present three time segments: The late 1800s, the mid-1900s, and the present. Probably the most difficult task was to do the last, so quickly are changes taking place around us. A case in point was the Sarnowski house in Glenville, once a summer home for an affluent Schenectady family. One month after I had taken the "today" picture, the place had been demolished and work started on a fast-food establishment. Similar happenings occurred on other subjects. Perhaps, by the time this book is in print, the presumably up-to-date scenes will be passé in some instances. (Readers are therefore advised to make notes at appropriate intervals.)

In doing this assignment, a native-born resident can become alternately depressed and elated over some of the more drastic changes which have occurred in his home town in recent years. Where a beautiful theater, railroad station, hotel or residence once stood, there might be a parking lot, partially filled. Then again, a stretch of erstwhile vacant fields and decaying farm buildings has suddenly become filled with modern housing, complete with families and a dividend for the future. Maybe it all balances out.

Another revelation in preparing this book was the fact that I have personally covered two parts of these three segments, the second and third. I saved many four-by five-inch negatives from my work as a press photographer in the forties and fifties. This meant that in duplicating scenes for the present, I was also treading the paths where I walked as a young man some four decades ago. That in itself makes me feel like Methuselah...but it's been worth the adventure.

—Larry Hart

# About the Author

**LARRY HART**
(March 17, 1920–February 10, 2004)

Larry Hart was not only an established author and journalist but also very much a "Renaissance Man" of his time who received many gifts from God in the form of extraordinary talents. Hart put all of those gifts and talents to work during his rich lifetime, including a writing talent in which he penned no less than fifteen books on local history of the Capital Region of upper New York State. This volume, written in 1987, was his tenth and one of which he was extremely proud.

Hart's long tenure with newspapers began when he worked as a part-time reporter while attending Mont Pleasant High School in the mid-1930s. He was a reporter-photographer for the *Schenectady Union-Star* and later county and political reporter for the *Schenectady Gazette* until becoming the editorial writer.

Until his death last year, Hart remained active as city and county historian of Schenectady, even until the late 1990s, lecturing and teaching continuing education classes at Union College and Schenectady County Community College on the subject of local history. His weekly column, "Tales of Old Dorp," concerning local history, was a beloved and widely read feature in the *Daily Gazette* for many years. The *Gazette* even now is reprising his past columns posthumously as a weekly item each Monday morning.

He attended public schools and Union College in Schenectady and was a World War II veteran with service in the Eighth Air Force, based in England. His widow, Ruth Brooks Hart, continues to live in their home in East Glenville, Schenectady County, and has two children, four grandchildren, and six great-grandchildren.